Spiritual Reading For
The Ecumenical Christian

30 Homilies And Sermons

Visit www.booksurge.com to order additional copies.

REV. ROBERT E. ALBRIGHT

SPIRITUAL READING FOR THE ECUMENICAL CHRISTIAN

30 Homilies And Sermons

2008

Spiritual Reading For The Ecumenical Christian

30 Homilies And Sermons

CONTENTS

1. Cosmos in the Bible   1
2. Israel: The Land   5
3. Israel: The Covenant   9
4. Covenant: The Jesus Movement   11
5. Christianity: The Jew/Gentile Question   15
6. Chosenness   19
7. The Promised Land   23
8. The Prophecy of Jeremiah   27
9. The Church and Judaism   31
10. "Nostra Aetate"   35
11. Anti-Semitism in the New Testament   41
12. Holocaust: Week of Remembrance   47
13. Interfaith Marriages   51
14. Sermon at a Jewish/Catholic Wedding   57
15. Homily at a Jewish/Catholic Wedding   59
16. Homily at a Catholic/Protestant Wedding   61
17. Homily at a Buddhist/Catholic Wedding   63
18. Good Friday Reflections   67
19. Rome and the Papacy   69
20. "Rerum Novarum"   73
21. John Henry Newman   79
22. The Role of the Laity in the Church   85
23. Priesthood of the Laity   89
24. The Intellectual Life of the Church   93
25. Annual Christian Unity Octave   97
26. Catholic and Lutheran Call for Unity   99
27. Reformation Sunday   103
28. The Temple—The Synagogue—The Church   109
29. The Four Marks of the Church   113
30. Evangelization   117

ACKNOWLEDGMENTS

I owe a great deal of gratitude to so many people whose influence, thoughts, and even words can be found throughout my homilies and sermons.

First to all the living and deceased members of the teams of liturgists and preachers who have journeyed with me over the years: Dominicuskerk and Studenten Ekklessia in Amsterdam; Loyola College, St. Matthew Parish, Emmaus Community, and Towson University Newman Center in Baltimore.

To my friends and colleagues who have had a profound effect on my growth in preaching: Bernard Huijbers, Huub Oosterhuis, Father Felix Malmberg, SJ, Sister Cleophas Costello, RSM, Dr. Bernard Nachbahr, Dr. Pastor Norman Beck, Mary Marousek, and Father Joseph Bonadio, SS.

To the scholarly works and teachings of Father Raymond Brown, SS, Father Edward Schillebeeckx, OP, Father Xavier Leon-Dufour, SJ, Father Roger Balducelli, OSFS, Bishop John Shelby Spong, Rabbi Joseph Telushkin, Abraham Heschel, and many others too numerous to name here.

To Agnieszka Balawejder, my friend and computer consultant, and to all those who sat through these homilies and sermons and encouraged me to put them into print.

A debt of thanks to you all!

INTRODUCTION / PREFACE

I am now retired, having served in the Roman Catholic Church as a brother of the Christian Schools for thirteen years and as a priest for the past thirty-five years. My ministries included teaching high school and serving as a houseparent in an orphanage while with the brothers, working as an associate pastor in two parish churches, and serving as campus minister at three colleges and universities since my ordination as a priest.

The following sermons and homilies are a sampling of my thirty-five years of preaching in the pulpit. I have adjusted many of these works to serve as spiritual reading for you, the reader. You will notice these writings are categorized as sermons and homilies—the difference being this: a **sermon** is a talk or essay that explores a particular religious topic or issue; a **homily** is a talk or essay that attempts to interpret a particular passage or passages of sacred Scripture in contemporary terms, applying it to the lives of the hearers or readers.

As you go through the pages ahead, you can spot a **homily** by the required reading passage(s) at the beginning of the essay. It will be necessary for the reader to have a Bible handy to read the cited passage(s) *before* embarking into the homily itself. The **sermons** have no particular Scripture required, but contain Scripture passages within the essay itself. Biblical quotations in this volume (unless otherwise noted) are taken from The New American Bible, 1988 translation.

Throughout the homilies and sermons, various noted spiritual writers will be quoted. Who they are and the sources of their words will be explained in the text itself, without the need for footnotes or the like. I hope this makes for easier reading without the distraction of going to the bottom of the page or to the rear of the book, causing the reader to lose track of thoughts, which are most important.

My hope in producing this little volume is not only to preserve some of the work I have done, but also to share it again with previous hearers and to expand to an even wider audience. In each of these pieces, I have attempted to challenge, inspire, and give meaning to the life of each of you, the readers. I pray that will happen! Thank you for opening yourself to me and all those whose words are contained herein.

Sincerely,
Father Bob Albright
November 2008

1.
COSMOS IN THE BIBLE

Readings: Deuteronomy 26:4-10 Psalm 114 Luke 4:1-13 Romans 10:8-13

We Christians have a long history and deep roots in the oldest traditions in the world. We have one foot in the great tradition of Israel, which comes to us through the Old Testament in the Bible. We have our other foot in the Gentile world of the past, which comes from both the Old and New Testaments of the Bible. Christianity is a composite of both the Jewish and Gentile traditions.

Our roots go back to Abraham and Sarah in the tradition of Israel and back to Adam and Eve in the Gentile tradition. Yes, we must remember Adam and Eve, Cain and Abel, Noah, and the people in the tower of Babel were all Gentiles. These were our Biblical Gentile ancestors. Our Biblical Jewish roots include Abraham and Sarah, Isaac and Rebecca, Jacob, Rachel, Leah and their twelve sons, Moses and the Exodus from Egypt, the judges, the kings, the prophets, and the Exile in Babylon.

"When Israel came away from Egypt...the mountains and hills... were jumping," because God gave Israel a land of its own, a Promised Land, flowing with milk and honey.

"When Israel came away from Egypt...the sea took flight...and the Jordan shrank back," because Egypt was slavery and Canaan was freedom.

"When Israel came away from Egypt...the rocks changed to springs and stones to water," because Egypt was HELL and the kingdom of Israel was HEAVEN!

To begin any understanding of our roots in Israel, we must first come to understand their view of the world back then.

The primitive understanding of the cosmos was a simple three-level or three-tiered universe. The top level was called HEAVEN. It was a composite of the sun, the moon, the stars, and sky and was the dwelling place of God. The middle level was called EARTH. The earth was a composite of land and water and was the dwelling place of living human beings. The bottom level was called SHEOL or the underworld. Sheol was a composite of land and fire and was the dwelling place of the dead.

You must keep this simple view of the universe in mind at all times when reading the Bible. Don't complicate this simple view with any of our more recent categories and philosophies and science. How we see the universe today is totally different than our ancestors perceived it. Let me explain!

The top level, HEAVEN, belonged to God. Only God lived in heaven. Heaven was the dwelling place of divinity. No people ever went to heaven, neither the living nor the dead.

The middle level, EARTH, belonged to the living. All human beings, while alive, inhabited the earth. However, God was apparently active on earth, since God was powerful enough to leave HEAVEN and enter into the history of living people.

The bottom level, SHEOL, belonged only to the dead. All human beings who lived on earth went to the land of the dead when they died. There in Sheol, they would lead a sub existence away from the living and away from God.

For the Hebrews of the Old Testament, the body and soul of a human being were inseparable. For them, the whole being (body and soul) went into the land of the dead at death. In other words, for the Jew in the Old Testament, there was no afterlife. "Afterlife" is a very late concept in the Bible and becomes a prominent theology only with the rise of Christianity.

Therefore, if the Jew of the Old Testament believed in no afterlife, this life is all they had. Life for the Hebrew was sacred, because there was no afterlife, only the land of the dead. Let's be clear here: The land of the dead was neither a place of punishment nor a place of reward—it was simply the place everyone (good and bad) went when life on earth ended. Keeping all this in mind, we can now begin to see some things in a clearer light.

First of all, imagine the faith of such a people, who lived life following God's Law with no reward of an afterlife or heaven or eternity with God. For the Jew of the Old Testament and the Jew of today, the Torah, the Law, is not the way to reward in an afterlife, but the way to a full and happy life in *this world*. Israel makes a covenant with God, not to secure happiness in the next world, but to live life to the fullest in *this world*. For Israel, *this world* is all there is for the living. The quality of life in *this world* is the whole reason for the Torah. The covenant between Israel and God is a pact to make *this* a better *world*, a kingdom where only God is king and peace reigns forever.

Secondly, if *this world* is all there is for the Jew, then we begin to see why the land becomes an issue from the very beginning up to the present day. God's part in the covenant is the promise of good land flowing with milk and honey—a sacred space where Israel could live according to the Torah in peace with all her neighbors. Egypt was not that land. Egypt was a land of slavery and oppression. Egypt was hell. The land of Canaan became the Promised Land where life in the Torah could be lived to the full—for Israel, the Promised Land is heaven!

To close, let me apply the brief information I have just given you with a Jewish perspective: In the mind of Israel, *this world* can be heaven, and *this world* can be hell. Heaven and hell are not reserved for the afterlife (because there is no afterlife), but are realities here in this life, on this earth, in *this world*. Slavery in Egypt was hell—freedom in Canaan was heaven. Living on foreign soil was hell—having a land of your own is heaven. Being alienated from God is hell—making a covenant with God is heaven.

And so, these are our roots. These are our beginnings. We came from this world. We grow in this world. We have become **this world**!

(Quotes from Psalm 114 above are taken from *Fifty Psalms* by Huub Oosterhuis, Herder and Herder, New York, 1969.)

2.

ISRAEL: THE LAND

Readings: Exodus 3:1-8, 13-15 Psalm 85 I Corinthians 10:1-6,10-12 Luke 13:1-9

In Deuteronomy we read, "God gave us this land flowing with milk and honey." In Genesis, God told Abraham, "To your descendents I give this land from the Wadi of Egypt to the Great River" (Gen.15:18). In the Book of Joshua, we read, "No longer was there manna for the Israelites because that year they could eat of the yield of the land of Canaan" (Josh. 5:12). In Exodus, God not only tells Moses, "I have come down to rescue (my people) from the hands of the Egyptians and lead them out of that land into a good and spacious land," but also tells Moses, "Remove the sandals from your feet, for the place where you stand is holy ground."

"The Holy Land"—that's not a term we Christians have coined for the near East, it is a term as old as Israel itself. God's part in the covenant with Israel was not just to release them from slavery, but give them a land of their own—a holy land. The land's holiness comes from the fact that it is given by God. Israel's holiness comes from the fact that they live on the land God has given them. In Biblical, Jewish thought, it is not what one does that makes one holy, but where one comes from that results in holiness.

And so we can begin to see why Israel established itself as a land again in 1948, and why it holds on to the land so energetically, refusing to give any of it up, even for Palestinian Arabs.

Let me explain further: Once Israel became a nation and settled itself in the land of Canaan (or Promised Land or Holy Land) it divided the land up among the twelve tribes. In Biblical times, being a Jew was equated with living on the land. Your portion of the land was given according to which tribe you belonged.

We understand all this even better if we look at the way Jews treated Gentiles in Biblical times, especially Gentiles who wanted to convert to Judaism (and there were lots of them). The person who lived off the land was called a "Nochri" or foreigner. The person who lived on the land, but was not Jewish, was called a "Ger" or resident alien. The person who converted to Judaism and lived on the land was called an "Ezrach" or full member. There was no ceremony for converting to Judaism, only one's relationship to the "land." The closer to Israel you were, the more a Jew you could be. One's status as a full member included both doing Jewish practices and living on the "land" (Ezrach). However, there was an intermediate step which required only living on the "land" (Ger). As a "Ger," one had legal status as a Jew. The foreigner or "Nochri" who did not live on the land was given no status as a Jew.

The land is central. The land is essential. The land is holy. The land is Israel!

And so, how do we apply these ideas? In what ways do Christians and Jews differ today?

A few examples might help answer these questions:

1. When we Christians sing the Psalms, we tend to theologize them. The Jews do not. For example, in Psalm 85 when it says, "Again and again you have favored your land, O God," the Christian thinks of land symbolically as all the earth or body of Christ or the Church; the Jew thinks of the land literally as Israel. In Psalm 126, when we sing, "When from our exile God takes us home again," the Christian again thinks of "exile" symbolically as this life and of "home" symbolically as heaven; the Jew, on the other hand, is literally thinking of "exile" as the diaspora or Babylonian captivity or living on foreign land, and of "home" as Israel, the holy land.

2. By the time we reach first century Palestine CE—the time of Jesus and his contemporaries—the land, the holy land, was scarred by Roman occupation and a large number of Gentiles living in the region of Galilee up north, Samaritans occupying the central regions with their own rituals and customs. Only Judea, in the south, was considered to be really Israel, the holy land. It is no wonder then, that the New Testament comment about Jesus could be made, "Can anything good come out of Nazareth?" (John 1:46). Nazareth was in Galilee, once a part of the holy land, but now the land of the pagan Gentiles.

We must *recognize* these differences between Jews and Christians, and hopefully we *understand* a little better, WHY!

(Citations from the Psalms above are taken from the translation of Huub Oosterhuis in *Fifty Psalms*, Herder and Herder, 1969.)

3.
ISRAEL: THE COVENANT

Readings: Joshua 5:9-12 Psalm 133 II Corinthians 5:17-21 Luke 15:1-3,11-32

As far as any recorded history can verify or any available prehistory evidence demonstrates, there have never been any ancient or primitive people who claimed to have a covenant with God, save Israel. Israel's claim to a covenant with God is unique. It is the only claim we know of prior to the rise of Christianity. The covenant between God and Israel stands in history as one of a kind, often envied by outsiders, misunderstood by some, scrutinized by all, even Jews.

How did this covenant come about? The ancient legend says—that in the beginning God offered the covenant to all the nations of the earth—only one people took God seriously and accepted the covenant; the others refused. Israel was that people who accepted. In the Bible, this legend is told in story form—Adam and Eve reject God's covenant; their son Cain rejects also; the people in Noah's day laugh in God's face; even the good Noah's descendents refuse a relationship with God. Finally, the Bible says, one man named Abram, a Hebrew, chooses God's offer to enter a relationship that would be a blessing, not only to him and his descendents, but eventually to all the nations of the earth. Through Abram, whom God calls Abraham, all of Israel is blessed. God chooses Abraham, because Abraham chooses God. The relationship is mutual. This relationship is called a covenant. According to the conditions of the covenant, every one of Abraham's descendents, by birth, are brought into this unique relationship with God.

What exactly are the elements or components of this covenant? The answer to this question has taken centuries to formulate. The covenant is basically a mutual agreement between Israel and God. On God's part it is an agreement to give blessing to every Jew, save them from their enemies, give them a land of their own, make them numerous and prosperous. On Israel's part it is an agreement to live according to the Torah—proclaiming the One God, following the commandments and making the earth a fit place for people to live. Israel's chief task of the covenant is to be a model for the world. Her task is and has always been to show that a relationship with God is the fullest possible way to live in this world. The covenant, therefore, is mutually productive, realistic, and practical, and establishes the clear identity of both parties involved. The covenant is a way of belonging, being in each other, a love affair. It is the longing for recognition, for peace, for satisfaction, for fulfillment—for blessing. It is the fullest possible means for both parties to keep life sacred.

Always remember, that Israel's guarantee is in this life and not in any hereafter. The purpose of the covenant always has been and remains a way to a full or meaningful life in this world. Israel's message to the world is that life is better lived if one lives it in a relationship with God. A healthy dependency on God is essential to the fullness of life. The covenant suggests that even God depends on people. God hopes in Israel. Israel hopes in God.

Finally, the covenant is eternal. It is "promise" par excellence. It is the way, the truth and the life. The story of the covenant is beautifully portrayed in Jesus' parable from the Gospel of Luke. The father = God; the elder son = Israel; the younger son = the Gentile Christians. As the legend goes, the Gentile world refused the covenant. Israel accepted it. But later, through Jesus, the Gentile world was welcomed by God back into the covenant—in fact, with open arms. Christians (the younger son) and Jews (the elder son) must learn to recognize that we are both in the same family, the same covenant, and we must learn how to live peaceably side by side. We must be more than brothers or siblings. We must become friends.

4.
COVENANT: THE JESUS MOVEMENT

Readings: Isaiah 43:16-21 Psalm 126 Philippians 3:8-14 John 8:1-11

In the earliest days of Christianity, long before it was called Christianity, while it was still the "Jesus Movement" or, as it was called, "The Way," also while the makeup of Christians was primarily Jewish people, Jesus was thought of in Jewish terms—that is—he was their Messiah. The covenant had not changed for them. It remained basically the same covenant God made with Abraham and ratified in Moses. Why? Because they were Jews! Jesus was a Jew. "The Twelve" were Jews. The earliest communities of disciples were Jews. They all were observant Jews; they continued to live the Torah, worship in the Temple, and celebrate Jesus in the breaking of bread in their houses on Sunday, while observing the Sabbath on Saturday. Get the picture?

When did this picture change? Well, actually, very early—so early we have no idea when exactly. All we know is that by the year 35 CE droves of Gentiles were entering Christianity. The mixture of Jews and Gentiles within Christianity was the factor that molded "The Way" into a worldwide movement.

As more and more Gentiles became baptized, Christianity took on a new look—was permeated with new ideas—found a new theology—and tried to justify the entry of Gentiles into the Church. All the old Jewish categories had to be rethought, reexamined—that included the covenant itself. For our purposes here, we will deal only with this one question of the covenant, since that covers all the issues that faced this new Church.

Now the question became—can Gentiles become Christians without becoming Jewish first? That is, are Gentiles bound by the covenant God made with Israel? Or, is God making a new covenant with Gentiles through Jesus? Or, is God allowing the Gentiles to enter the covenant made with Israel, not through Torah, but through faith in Jesus?

To answer these questions, our ancestors in faith went to God's Word in the Scripture for help. Passages, as we read in Isaiah, resound with new meaning, "Remember not the events of the past, the things of long ago consider not; see, I am doing something new! Now it springs forth, do you not perceive it?" An echo of this can be found in the prophet Jeremiah where he says, even more clearly, "The days are coming, says the Lord, when I will make a new covenant with the house of Israel and Judah...I will place my law within them, and write it upon their hearts" (Jeremiah 31:31-33).

As the early Christian writers purged the Scripture to look for some sign from God about this new Gentile phenomenon, it was remembered that God's promise to Abraham in the Book of Genesis was that **all** the nations of the earth would find blessing through him. The author of the Gospel of Matthew, who concentrated on this text from Genesis, by the year 80 CE when he writes his Gospel, has justified the entry of the Gentiles into the Church as having been God's plan even before the world was made. Thus when Matthew and the other New Testament writers pictured God's plan for the Gentiles, it was the same picture we see in Psalm 126—the Gentiles, "exiles" since the sins of Adam and Eve and Cain and Babel, are now being brought "home" again, that is, into a covenant with God, but through Jesus. This "dream" became eventually an all-Gentile Church, an all-Gentile religion. By the end of the first century of the Common Era, Christianity had one foot in the world of Judaism and one foot in the Gentile world (both feet solidly rooted in both worlds).

St. Paul sums all this up in the Letter to the Philippians, "I have come to rate all as loss in the light of the surpassing knowledge of my Lord Jesus Christ. For his sake I have forfeited everything...the justice I possess is that which comes through faith in Christ. It has its origin in God and is based on faith." Writing to Gentiles in Philippi, Paul is justifying their place in the covenant. What he is willing to forfeit for them is the Torah. Their faith in Christ is their justification for entrance into the covenant—they need not observe the Torah.

And now all the Gentiles return to God, through Jesus, "singing, sheaves on our shoulders."

(Quotes from Psalm 126 above are from the translation of Huub Ososterhuis, *Fifty Psalms,* Herder and Herder, 1969.)

5.
CHRISTIANITY: THE JEW/GENTILE QUESTION

Our roots as Christians in the Gentile world now need some attention. Let us take a look at the whole issue of baptism—not only as a sacrament, but also its relationship to the whole question of being Christian. If St. Augustine were here to dialogue with us, he would underscore the need for baptism as a requisite for salvation. Augustine coined the term "original sin" and saw baptism as a removal of this inherited condition. For Augustine and the entire Christian Church (up to Vatican II), the "original sin" of Adam and Eve, which resulted in death and alienation from God, was inherited by every human being born into this world. Only baptism could remove it. This older theology taught that by birth we are sinners, therefore, a new birth in the waters of baptism is necessary to reconcile us with the life prepared for us by Jesus in heaven. Most of us grew up with these teachings and thus we saw the need to baptize infants, who otherwise would not be reconciled to God should they die before they could be baptized by their own volition.

Let us begin with that term "original sin." "Original," yes. "Sin," I'm not so sure! Let's go back to the story—God gives Adam and Eve life and the Garden of Eden, enough to eat and all the pleasures of living. All God asks in return is obedience to one commandment—not to eat of the tree of the knowledge of good and evil. The first covenant—the "original" covenant—the first relationship between the human and divine! Each party has his or her part to do to keep the covenant, to keep the relationship—God provides; Adam and Eve obey—only one commandment. God should do more since God is divine and divine is infinite. Adam and Eve were human and limited, thus one commandment was enough (and apparently, even too much).

When Adam and Eve disobeyed the only commandment that bound them to the covenant, they broke their relationship with the divine. This was not a sin, but it was their choice. If they could break their part of the covenant, then so could God. God's part was to provide them with all the life they needed—and so God gave up the divine requirement of a happy life—therefore, pain, suffering, sin, and death were the results. That they both (human and divine) gave up the covenant resulted in no covenant with God for all the descendents of Adam and Eve. And this is what Augustine called "original sin." However, this was not a sin. Sin was the result of this original break, not the cause. And so we need another term. "Original sin" will no longer do.

Christianity has always seen the role of Jesus as the restorer of that original covenant. Jesus, a Jew, one who naturally came into the covenant Abraham made with God, now comes as *the Way* for all nations to reconcile themselves with God and restore that original covenant. The first Christians (who were all Jews) saw this mystery unfold before them in the life, death, and resurrection of this Jew, Yeshua of Nazareth. For Jews, the covenant came with birth. All Jews are naturally born into a covenant with God.

The first Christians (who were all Jews) soon became faced with Gentile converts to Christianity. Gentiles were not Jews by birth. How could Gentiles become members of the covenant? Two choices: by becoming Jews or by faith in Jesus Christ. Faith in Jesus became *the Way* for all Gentiles to restore a covenant with God. And baptism became the sign or sacrament or supernatural birth into the covenant for all Gentiles. For the Gentile, baptism is the initiation into the New Covenant or New Testament of Jesus Christ.

Let me reiterate more clearly: A Jew naturally enters the covenant at birth, simply by coming through the water of the womb. A Gentile supernaturally enters the covenant (not at birth), but by being reborn through the water of baptism. Baptism is the washing away of being children of Adam and Eve and siblings of Cain and raises us to a new life as the children of Abraham and brothers and sisters in Christ Jesus.

And so, baptism is not our entrance into heaven, but into the covenant here on earth. It is an entrance into the Church, the visible community of the Gentile covenant above, below, and on the earth. Thus, worrying about an unbaptized baby or child dying is no longer a concern. For baptism doesn't get us into heaven, it gets us into the covenant and the covenant is lived here on this earth.

And so, baptism is an equinox, a turning point for us Gentiles. We turn into the youth of a new life in Christ; we turn into the age-old covenant with God; we turn toward each other in the community we call Church—so we can see how close we are and celebrate each other!

6.
CHOSENNESS

Readings: Isaiah 66:18-21 Hebrews 12:5-7,11-13 Luke 13:22-30

How odd
of God
to choose
the Jews
Ogden Nash

In a simple outline form below, I list many religious groups throughout Western civilization that have claimed to be chosen by God:

- In 1000 BCE **Israel** experiences an awareness of being chosen.

- In 500 BCE Text above from Isaiah—"All nations" will come to Israel (Jerusalem) the seat of chosenness.

- In 35 CE **Christianity** sees itself as the new Israel and rejects Judaism as no longer God's chosen. Christians are now chosen.

- In 80 CE Text above from Luke—everyone will enter the kingdom even before Israel.

- In 625 CE Muhammed dictates the Koran in which **Islam** supersedes both Judaism and Christianity.

- In 637 CE Muslims capture Jerusalem from Jews and Christians, and see this as a form of God's favor and choice.

- In 1830 CE   Joseph Smith and friends found the **Mormons** or Church of The Latter-Day Saints to supersede Christianity and reinterpret it. Mormons see themselves as the elect who will enter heaven.

- In 1871 CE   Founding of the **Jehovah's Witnesses** as a response to the Book of Revelation, which promises that only a certain number will be saved in the end-time—the Jehovah's Witnesses claim to be these saved ones! The elect! The chosen!

- In 1910 CE   The rise of **Christian fundamentalism** in reaction to mainline Christianity (Protestant and Catholic). They see themselves as the only true Christians because they take the Bible literally. Their being reborn is a form of election, of being chosen.

Do you see the pattern?
Who's next?
Who will come along and replace the fundamentalists?!

The concept of being chosen is not an exclusive idea necessarily. Today, Jews are even saying that there are other ways, others elected or chosen. Being chosen means being given a specific task—not being better or separate. God has chosen different people to do different things. Anything else has led to elitism.

However, Jesus tried to say that all people are equal in God's sight, all are chosen, all are saved.

Any religion with "chosenness" has a fundamental problem that it must see and deal with!

The problem is not with a God who chooses (e.g., Israel *and* Egypt, Christians *and* Jews, Mormons *and* Christians, etc.), but the human misunderstanding of what it means to be chosen (e.g., Israel *over* Egypt, Christians *over* Jews, Mormons *over* Christians, etc.).

When God, the infinite, limitless mystery, chooses, we humans, with our limitations and finiteness often do not know how to handle it. We pitch ourselves against each other rather than seeing ourselves as complementary. We humans must learn to live with the tension between being created in God's image and likeness, and at the same time being different. How can we be different and the same all at the same time? This is the mystery of who we are.

Rather than fight among ourselves, we should:
Thank God for this paradox;
Thank God for this mystery;
Thank God we are created in God's image;
Thank God we are chosen;
Thank God we are different from others who are also **chosen!**

7.
THE PROMISED LAND

Readings: Isaiah 35:4-7a Psalm 146 James 2:1-5 Mark 7:31-37

A s you know so well, the enslaved Hebrews were led out of Egypt by Moses to seek a promised land. They spent numerous years of strife wandering in the desert as they struggled to reach this Promised Land. With violence, they stormed the walls of Jericho and entered the Promised Land, and built a magnificent city and a temple for Yahweh. It was precisely through all of these events that Israel discovered who Yahweh was: a liberating God. The covenant ratified by Moses, the Promised Land, and the priesthood were all signs of God's presence and God's liberating actions.

Then, after many centuries of battles and disagreements with Gentile enemies, the Babylonian armies came to destroy the temple and whisk the Hebrews off to Babylon, where they once again found themselves in captivity. Only the royalty, as representing Yahweh, the noblemen, landowners, and skilled artisans of the Hebrews were taken into exile, where they remained for some fifty years, while the poor and peasant class of Hebrews were left behind, since they were of no value to the captors. This event was devastating for Israel. The tangible signs of Yahweh's presence were destroyed and taken away. They faced an inevitable inward crisis: where and who is this Yahweh who once liberated us? We, ourselves, would be faced with such a question if all our Christian signs were taken from us—if our churches were burned to the ground, our priests murdered, our pope and bishops taken into captivity. We also would ask: what kind of a God would do this to us?

While in Babylon, prophets arose among the Hebrews who challenged the ways they understood themselves and Yahweh. After much personal inward conflict and struggle with this whole experience, the prophet Isaiah spoke the prophecy in the passage above: He spoke to those whose hearts were frightened saying, "Here is your God, he comes with vindication...he comes to save you...the ears of the deaf will be cleared, the tongue of the dumb will sing...streams will burst forth in the desert." A new awareness of God develops. They become conscious of "Yahweh" who lives in his people. He no longer lives in the temple of fancy; yet, he still exists among his people, speaking through the prophets, promising liberation once again.

The center of gravity of Israelite life, their national and religious consciousness, was moved to Babylon. And through this significant event, the people became aware that the Promised Land was not a place, some territory, but that it was a hope for a future, a stability, a life where they could live in peace and freedom.

This Promised Land was once sought through violence, through hatred and prejudices toward Gentiles, through exclusive lifestyles, all of which Yahweh seemed to favor. BUT this is how THEY conceived him. With the prophets of the exile, and especially Isaiah, a whole new concept of God and his relationship to people arises. But even more important, a whole new concept of people's relationship to other people evolves.

No longer will the Promised Land or Kingdom of God be accomplished through violence, but through peace. No longer through hatred, but through love. No longer through prejudice, but through openness to all people of all languages, sexes, beliefs, and colors. This is the future Isaiah envisions, and the future lived by Jesus Christ.

This prophecy of Isaiah—hope expressed in the midst of captivity— is like finding a green twig in wintertime. The way of the man from Nazareth brings this prophecy to life, so alive that the blind and the deaf know him; so alive that a tomb could not contain him. His way was one of peace, love, and openness, the way each of us must go. The Pharisee, the beggar, the Samaritan, the rich, the poor, the ugly, the Jew, the Gentile, white, black, the beautiful, the adulteress...all have room in his life, in his Kingdom.

Any sort of prejudice and racism would tear at the very heart of this Kingdom. For this is its heart: That there is one God, and no one race alone can claim him—no one nationality alone can own him—no one religion alone can possess him. He is Father of all. All good comes from him so that men, women, and children are brothers and sisters called to imitate him, their Father. To exclude anyone from this Kingdom on some pretext of race, nationality, or religion would make human groups radically unequal, and Christianly speaking, one could call this atheism, for it is to deny that God is God. How, then, can we say, "Our Father," if we exclude some people from the quality of "brothers and sisters," and therefore, children of God? Nothing is easier than to connect a certain number of faults and characteristics, which displease or annoy us, with the color of a skin, the shape of a face, the use of a language, the images of a style of life different from our own. Thus, the duty of the Christian, and indeed, of every person who wants to preserve a genuine brotherly and sisterly sense of the other, is to be critical about the false representations attributed to a race or nationality, religion or sexual minority, and to build up in oneself by true information and personal contacts the sense of unity that is the heart of the Kingdom spoken of in the Gospel.

The Promised Land and kingdom of God are founded on love of our neighbor, and rest on a certain sensitivity toward others, with the absence of contempt and mistrust, and the presence of openness, and a desire to understand and share. This openness and sharing could even lead us to see that the Promised Land is an integrated world where men and women, black and white, homosexual and heterosexual, Catholic and Protestant, Jew and Gentile, conservative and liberal, can all live in harmony as the people of God. To be a racist, to exclude, to be petty-minded, is to enslave and hold captive; to turn the Promised Land into Egypt and Babylon, rather than to build the Kingdom.

And so my friends, become people of God, go with Jesus, away from the crowds, let him put his fingers into your ears...and listen as he groans: "Ephphatha...Be opened!"

8.
THE PROPHECY OF JEREMIAH

Readings: Jeremiah 31:31-34 Psalm 51 Hebrews 5:7-9 John 12:20-23

The days are coming, says the Lord, when I will make a new covenant with the house of Israel and the house of Judah...I will place my law within them, and write it upon their hearts" (Jeremiah 31).

For the past two millennia, the Christian Church (Gentiles) have interpreted this passage as belonging to itself, as referring to Christianity itself, as the New Testament. Yet, if we look carefully at this passage, this new covenant is promised by God to the house of Israel and the house of Judah—not to the Gentiles. The Christian Church has been Gentile for all but the first seventy years of its two-thousand-year history. This passage from Jeremiah could not possibly be referring to Christianity. This passage from Jeremiah has yet to be fulfilled.

The Jews have just embarked on the fourth millennium since King David established the nation of Israel. We Christians have just embarked on the third millennium since the birth of Jesus. Perhaps our third millennium and the Jews' fourth millennium will be the time when this prophecy of Jeremiah will come to pass and be the seed that will produce much fruit.

That fruit could be the Jewish recognition of the validity of Christianity, and the Christian recognition that Judaism is not obsolete and superseded by the New Testament...that the Old Covenant does not preclude a new one and that the New Testament does not replace the Old...that the Old and New Testaments are different ways ordained by God of keeping the same covenant...that following the Torah is the Way, the Truth, and the Life for a Jew and that following the Gospel is the

Way, the Truth, and the Life for a Christian and that these two "Ways" are mysteriously linked in the person of Jesus.

The third and fourth millenniums, then, could be the "right time" to discover that…
- For Jews and Christians alike, Yeshua, bar Yosef, was, is, and always will be a Jew.
- For Jews and Christians alike, Yeshua, son of Mary, was, is, and always will be a human being.
- For Jews and Christians alike, Jesus of Nazareth was, is, and always will be God's prophet among us.
- For Jews and Christians alike, Jesus, descendant of Abraham, was, is and always will be the source of God's blessing to all the Gentiles.
- For Jews and Christians alike, Jesus, son of David, was, is, and always will be God's Anointed.
- For Christians and Jews alike, the God of Jesus was, is, and always will be the God of Israel.
- For Christians and Jews alike, the God of Israel was, is, and always will be the God of all creation.
- For Christians and Jews alike, the God of all creation was, is, and always will be the maker of covenants.
- For Christians and Jews alike, the God of the covenant was, is, and always will be ONE AND THE SAME GOD, for Christians and Jews alike!

My hope, then, is that this new millennium will see the hopes and dreams of Pope John XXIII and Rabbi Abraham Heschel come to fruition in a new covenant between Christians and Jews…
as
we speak to each other
openly, honestly, sincerely, respectfully, truthfully
as
Jew speaks to Christian
Christian speaks to Jew
Old Testament speaks to New Testament
New Testament speaks to Old Testament

Torah speaks to Gospel
Gospel speaks to Torah
and
"Heart speaks to Heart"

And why can this hope of mine be possible? Because of Jeremiah's prophecy:

"I will make a new covenant with the house of Israel and the house of Judah... and write it upon their **Hearts**."

9.

THE CHURCH AND JUDAISM

Readings: Deuteronomy 6:2-5 Psalm 19 Hebrews 7:23-28 Mark 12:28-34

Given the commandments and the call of the Scripture above—to worship the God of Israel—how does a Christian respond to being Israel?

How does the Church define herself in both the Old and New Testaments?

How do we see ourselves in relation to Judaism today?

In other words: When the Scripture says—"Hear, O Israel"—who is Israel today?

A brief history of Israel will help us understand ourselves as Israel. It all begins with Abraham who had two sons, Ishmael and Isaac. It is through the line of Isaac that the nation of Israel begins. Ishmael will come back later in our story. Isaac becomes the father of Jacob whose name is changed to Israel by the angel who struggles with him in a dream. Jacob (Israel) has twelve sons who eventually become the twelve tribes of Israel as they multiply and grow in population. Their history is varied with ups and downs. They go into slavery in Egypt and are liberated by Moses. They become a nation under David and enter civil war under Rehoboam, son of Solomon.

Around the year 722 BCE the Assyrians, who have become a world power, come and smash the Northern Kingdom of Israel destroying ten of the twelve tribes. We have no archeological evidence of any remains of the ten tribes. They are lost—perhaps forever. Only two tribes remain in the Southern Kingdom of Judah—the tribes of Benjamin and Judah (*Yehudah* in Hebrew, *Jew* in English). The larger of these two tribes is Judah. The Babylonians come to world power and in the year 597 BCE destroy Judah, the king, the temple, and Jerusalem and lead the tribes into exile in Babylon. Sixty years later when Persia ascends to world power, she conquers Babylon and returns all the captives to their homeland. The only tribes that now remain (Judah and Benjamin) return to Israel to rebuild. From this time onward, Israel becomes known as "The Jews."

Judaism develops into many sects and by the time of Jesus there are at least four major sects detectable under Roman occupation. Jesus comes along as a reform movement in Judaism, which is eventually called the Jesus Movement, the Way, and later, Christianity. The first Christians were Jews. Jesus was a Jew. Christianity eventually prospers and finds its home in the Gentile world, but originally was a reform movement in Judaism.

Knowing all of this, let us return to the questions I proposed above and begin to see how we Christians fit into the mystery of Israel. Also remember that the historical lineage of Ishmael returns in history to form the nation of Islam and the Muslin faith through Muhammed around 625 CE. All three monotheistic religions come from the same great grandfather, Abraham.

Therefore, let us imagine the three monotheistic religions as a tree with Abraham at its roots, Israel as the trunk of the tree, and Christians and Jews and Muslims with their many denominations as various branches on the tree. No branch is greater or better or right or wrong. They are simply branches—all part of the same tree, having the same roots and foundation. Consider, therefore, creation as a garden of many trees. Our tree is called "Israel." There are pagan trees, oriental trees, Native American trees, etc. All trees are of God's creation.

And so, we are Israel at our roots. We share those roots with all sorts of other people and religions, especially the Jews. Today, we recognize in our new view that there are many ways to God, ours being one among many. We no longer see the need to convert or proselytize or force our way on others. We recognize other ways as valid as our own. Listen to the words of the Roman Catholic Church on this matter taken from the document of Vatican II, forty-three years ago:

The Catholic Church rejects nothing that is true and holy in these religions. She regards with sincere reverence those ways of conduct and of life, those precepts and teachings which, though differing in many aspects from the ones she holds and sets forth, nonetheless often reflect a ray of that Truth which enlightens all people. Indeed, she proclaims, and ever must proclaim Christ "the way, the truth, and the life" (John 14:6), in whom people may find the fullness of religious life, in whom God has reconciled all things to Himself...No foundation, therefore, remains for any theory or practice that leads to discrimination between person and person or people and people, so far as their human dignity and the rights flowing from it are concerned...The Church reproves as foreign to the mind of Christ, any discrimination against people or harassment of them because of their race, color, condition of life, or religion. On the contrary, following in the footsteps of the holy apostles Peter and Paul, this sacred synod ardently implores the Christian faithful to "maintain good fellowship among the nations" (I Peter 2:12), and, if possible, to live for their part in peace with all people, so that they may truly be children of the Father who is in heaven ("*Nostra Aetate*" Paragraphs 6, 19, and 20).

Therefore, when Jesus says, "Hear, O Israel," he means you and me (Christians) called to not only believe in the God of Israel, but to believe in a God who gives both Jews and Christians the same way to live:

Hear, O Israel! The Lord our God is Lord alone!
Therefore, you shall love the Lord your God
with all your heart, with all your soul, with all your mind,
and with all your strength.
You shall love your neighbor as yourself.
There is no other commandment greater than these.

10.
"NOSTRA AETATE"
October 28, 1965

(This sermon was delivered to the Beth Am Reform Congregation of Judaism at the Shabbas Torah Service, March 16, 1991, in Baltimore, Maryland.)

In our time, when day by day humankind is being drawn closer together, and the ties between different peoples are becoming stronger, the Church examines more closely her relationship to non-Christian religions. In her task of promoting unity and love among people, indeed among nations, she considers above all in this declaration what people have in common and what draws them to fellowship."

With these words, twenty-five years ago, the Fathers of the Second Vatican Council began the document, "Nostra Aetate," which was to change the relationship between the Roman Catholic Church and Jews, Muslims, Hindus, Buddhists, and all non-Christian religions (hopefully) for all time!

In the spirit of Pope John XXIII and the council's mandate of "Aggiornamento," windows and doors, locked for centuries, were thrown open and fresh air once again filled the world of Christianity!

Coming as it did, only twenty years after the Second World War and the Holocaust, Vatican II was a clear response to the changing theology that emerged as a result of this devastating world event in the Christian and non-Christian communities alike.

Therefore, in an attempt to reverse almost two thousand years of isolation, hostility, and competition, which led to the monstrosity we call "the Holocaust," Vatican II set in motion new theology that created new relationships with other Christians, as well as non-Christians.

To keep these entities separate (a necessity by the very nature of these categories, Christian and non-Christian), separate documents emerged, one governing the relations between Roman Catholics and other Christians, and "Nostra Aetate," the document governing the relations between Roman Catholics and non-Christian religions.

The scope of "Nostra Aetate," then, is larger than just the relations between Jews and Catholics. First, there is a prologue that draws together all religions that seek the one God. Secondly, there is a section dealing with Catholics' relations with Eastern religions and Muslims. In this section, the document makes a statement typical of the spirit that runs throughout. Referring to Buddhists and Hindus, the document reads: "The Catholic Church rejects nothing that is true and holy in these religions." The third and most major section of the document is the section on the relations of Catholicism with Judaism. I will turn to this section in a moment in more detail. Finally, there is an epilogue stressing the need for unity and peace among all peoples and religions, characteristically found in this passage: "The Church reproves as foreign to the mind of Christ, any discrimination against people or harassment of them because of their race, color, condition of life, or religion. On the contrary...this sacred synod ardently implores the Christian faithful...to live for their part in peace with all people."

And now, let me turn to that segment of "Nostra Aetate" that brings me here today and in which I find special joy—the relationship between Judaism and Catholicism, between Jews and Catholics, between brothers and sisters who have been engaged in a family feud for the past 1,960 years.

And so, what exactly does this document say about the relationship between Jews and Catholics? Let me do three things to convey this best: first, I will simply state as objectively as I can what the document itself says; second, I will then offer some commentary on the document; last, I will suggest some direction we might wish to pursue in the future.

The document or declaration (as we call it in Catholic circles) takes five extraordinary, significant, and totally new directions in the way Catholics should view their relations with Jews:

1. That Judaism is a valid religion on its own; with or without Christianity. That the promises God made have not been rescinded, and therefore converting Jews to Christianity is arrogant and even goes against the nature of the God in whom we place our faith. How can Christians trust in the God of Israel (as we do) if that God goes back on the promises he already made to Israel?

2. That Christians must not view Judaism as less than itself—with Christianity being the fulfillment of all that is "Old Testament"—in other words, supersessionistic Christian attitudes are condemned by the Church. We no longer see the "New Testament" as a better covenant, but the same covenant as that given to Israel, now made accessible to us Gentiles through the life, death, and resurrection of Jesus, whom we call "the Christ."

3. That the ancient, unhistorical and mindless charge that all Jews are responsible for the death of Jesus should be stricken from the hearts, minds, and verbal debates of Christians. "Nostra Aetate" reminds the Christian Community of its own theology, which contradicts this fictitious charge by saying: "Besides, as the Church has always held and holds now, Christ underwent his passion and death freely, because of the sins of people and out of infinite love."

4. That the Church "decries hatred, persecutions, displays of anti-Semitism, directed against Jews at any time and by anyone." That the teaching of contempt (so prevalent in Christianity against Judaism for centuries) be replaced by the teaching of love.

5. And finally, a clarion call by the Church to foster mutual understanding and respect between Christians and Jews, which can only come through common biblical and theological studies as well as dialogue on every level of our two communities.

And now permit me some commentary on this document, which is already twenty-five years old.

If this document were written today, it would be significant. Imagine how much more twenty-five years ago! Can you remember the world between 1962 and 1965? Clearly, this declaration is the handiwork of visionaries such as your own beloved Abraham Heschel and Dr. Joseph Lichten (May their memory be a blessing.) and our own beloved Pope John XXIII (May he rest in peace.).

Because there is no similar document in the history of the Church's tradition—this can be considered a foundation document. It is not built on any tradition or documents of the past. It is totally new. It is a document on which we now must build the future, for our own sake, our children's sake, for God's sake.

"Nostra Aetate" (like most Catholic documents) avoids extremes. It does not say any religion is as good as another. Nor does it say that Catholicism is the only true religion. Somewhere in the balance we can find one another; we can find the truth; we can find God.

This milestone document, intended for the worldwide Catholic community calls for a change of heart, for a conversion, for a whole new way of defining what it means to be Christian, what it means to be Jewish— and that neither definition diminishes the identity of the other.

One criticism of this document that keeps occurring is the brevity of this statement that doesn't develop all its ideas fully. Perhaps this is due to the fact I pointed to earlier—that this is a foundation document. The need is to flesh out the issues with further documentation using "Nostra Aetate" as a basis from which to operate.

However, its greatest critics decry the lack of repentance and search for forgiveness within the document itself. Again, perhaps this is due to another fact we have to keep in mind—the audience of the declaration is the worldwide Catholic Community. The council obviously saw no need to ask Catholics for forgiveness for what was perpetrated against the Jews by Christians over the centuries.

On the other hand, my presence among you today is an attempt to build on "Nostra Aetate" by sharing the document with the Jewish community in hopes that together we can continue its efficacy into the future of both our communities. And also, my presence is a small attempt on the part of the Catholic Community to seek reconciliation and beg forgiveness for whatever wrongs Christians in the past have done to Jews, and to plead with you to be merciful to us, for we have sinned.

Finally, may I close by suggesting what still needs to be done: on the part of Christians, and Catholics most especially—that the declaration "Nostra Aetate" be taken to heart—that it be preached from pulpits and taught in our classrooms—that it be the source for adult education programs and sessions of dialogue among Catholics, as well as all Christians and Jews.

On the part of the Jewish Community—there is a need for you to abandon your legitimate suspicion of Christians and begin to place some trust in us as we try to reverse the past. Regaining trust is no easy thing, as the Christians of today are well aware. My Christian ancestors perpetrated violence, hatred and contempt. From the first century of the Common Era polemics of anti-Judaism to the anti-Semitism of the first half of the twentieth century, Christian behavior and thought has been deplorable against Jews.

In the face of all this, my contemporary counterparts and myself wish to build a new life between Christians and Jews—a life that does not forget the dark past, but uses it as a forceful impetus toward a future world where Christians, Jews, and all "...the elect will be united in the Holy City, the city ablaze with the glory of God, where the nations will walk in God's light."

Sha'alu Shalom Shalayim!
Shabbat Shalom!

*All quoted translations of "Nostra Aetate" above are from The National Catholic Welfare Conference.

11.
ANTI-SEMITISM IN THE NEW TESTAMENT

(This sermon was delivered at the opening Sunday liturgy at the Towson University Newman Center annual Week of Remembrance commemorating the victims of the Holocaust.)

Reading: John 20:19-31

What does one say about the murder of eleven million human beings?

Did it really happen? YES!

Could it happen again? YES!

Who would be party to such a gigantic crime? Madmen? Criminals? Mentally deranged people? Warped consciences? NO!

For over fifty years now scholars around the world have been analyzing and scrutinizing and studying this catastrophic phenomenon called "The Holocaust." And the most frightening discovery that has been made about this outrageous event is that it was not perpetrated by a madman or any mentally deranged individuals. It was accomplished by ordinary sane people, intellectuals, like you and me. The most horrific discovery of the past fifty years of research is that you and I are capable of perpetrating such a holocaust. In other words—it is within the capacity of the most ordinary human being to bring down destruction, murder, and death, not only on other human beings, but upon the entire planet.

How is this possible?

Well, it starts small, maybe even naively or innocently at first, and then it builds unseen, sinister, undetected, here, there, and eventually it breaks loose when we are no longer capable of controlling it!

While reading the Gospel above, you yourself heard the seeds of contempt in your own Scripture, written almost two thousand years ago. Did you even notice it? "For fear of **the Jews**" (John 20:19). Would anyone even think that his or her sacred Scripture would contain a teaching of contempt? Yet, it is there in the New Testament, as well as in other sacred books of the Jews and Muslims and Mormons and others (Cf. *Mature Christianity* by Norman Beck, pages 21-28).

However, let me confine us to our own New Testament, where we hear passages like: "The God of our ancestors raised Jesus, though **you** had him killed by hanging him on a tree" (Acts 5:30). "And the **whole people** said in reply: 'His blood be on us and on our children'" (Matthew 27:25). "The Chief Priests and Scribes were seeking a way to put him to death, for they were afraid of the people" (Luke 22:2).

Let's begin by citing these passages as clear teachings of contempt by Christian Jews against Pharisaical Jews of the first century. Jesus died around the year 33 CE. Fifty strenuous years followed for both Christian Jews and Jews who remained in the tradition of the Pharisees. It was during that time, around the year 70 CE, that the Romans destroyed Jerusalem and the temple. Both Christian Jews and Pharisaical Jews were uprooted and dispersed all over the Roman Empire. Because of this, there was never a chance for reconciliation between Jewish Christians and other Jews in that period of turmoil. Both Jewish communities went their separate ways and have never reconciled until modem times.

When the Gospels and the Acts of the Apostles were written around the end of the first century CE, the Romans were a threat to the fledgling Jewish Christian communities. Attempts were made by Christian Jews in the New Testament to shift the blame for Jesus' death away from the Romans and on to the Jews (as we heard in these passages I just quoted). The period in which the New Testament was written (75-100 CE) was a time of intense persecution by the Romans toward Christianity. Judaism itself was a legal religion in the Roman Empire at that time. But Christian Jews were seen and treated as "outside" Judaism and became the target of Roman hostility. To protect themselves, the writers of the New Testament went soft on the Roman involvement in Jesus' death and shifted the blame onto the Pharisaical Jews—even though crucifixion was clearly a Roman death penalty.

For most of our history as a Christian community, we were not aware of the conclusions of modern biblical scholarship. Therefore, Christians have taken the entire New Testament literally and slowly over time built an unwarranted animosity against all Jews. And when Christianity became the state religion for all of Europe around the year 313 CE, persecutions of Jews became routine and unquestioned in many circles.

It was this religious climate all over the continent of Europe for sixteen hundred years that slowly festered into Nazi concentration camps and fed the flames of Auschwitz. Christian anti-Judaism was **not** the cause—but contributed to the slaughter of the Jews in World War II! There were, of course, many components that came together and produced the Holocaust and the Second World War as we know it, but we as a Christian people must never forget the foundation our religion laid for the building up of this travesty. Christian anti-Judaism sprang from the New Testament itself as if it were God who was blaming all Jews for the death of Jesus.

The Roman Catholic Church, after almost two thousand years, came to its senses about thirty-six years ago when it proclaimed the document at the Second Vatican Council, entitled, "Nostra Aetate" ("In Our Time"). This "Declaration on the Relation of the Church to Non-Christian Religions" makes this statement:

> True, the Jewish authorities and those who followed their lead pressed for the death of Christ; still, what happened in His passion cannot be charged against all the Jews, without distinction, then alive, nor against the Jews of today. Although the Church is the new people of God, the Jews should not be presented as rejected or accursed by God, as if this followed from Holy Scriptures ("Nostra Aetate" #4f).

And now, you begin to see the danger in reading any Scripture literally. When we read these passages from the Gospels and Acts of the Apostles, literally for hundreds of years, we upheld a teaching of contempt against all Jews, because that was what Scripture said. However, since the modern biblical scholarship of the last century, we have come to learn that these passages were contrived by the early Church to protect itself against the Romans—who really **did** kill Jesus! And who would not hesitate to kill Christians for anti-Roman statements in their Scripture.

And so, what should we do? Dr. Norman Beck, a Lutheran pastor and biblical scholar makes the following suggestions:

> If we will take seriously the statements of Christian groups such as the World Council of Churches since 1948, the Lutheran World Federation and the House of Bishops of the Protestant Episcopal Church since 1964, the Second Vatican Council of the Roman Catholic Church since 1965, the Lutheran Council in the U.S.A. since 1971, and the American Lutheran Church since 1974, we will repudiate the defamatory anti-Jewish polemic of the New Testament not only in word, but also in deed. Under the guidance of the Spirit of God in translations of the New Testament intended for popular use, we will "prune" into footnote status its most viciously defamatory particles. In other instances, in which the polemic is less virulent, we will use circumlocution and translation according to the sense of the text in order to reduce emphasis upon the Jews, Judaism, and the Pharisees...We will be more selective in our choice of lectionary texts, providing readings (at Mass) that are less blatantly anti-Jewish (*Mature Christianity*, page 285).

We Christians have a wealth of sacred Scripture that is not filled with polemics or teachings of contempt against anyone. Let us learn to discriminate between the Word of God and the words of humans found in the Bible. Let us commit ourselves as inheritors of both the Old and New Testaments to become educated in modern biblical scholarship so as to use Scripture wisely, be able to competently teach our children, and ultimately become honest to the Word of God, which calls to us: "Hine ma tov uma naim, shevet achim gam yachad" ("Behold how wonderful and good it is when brothers and sisters dwell together in unity").

And so, what has brought us here today? What has brought us

full circle from having Jewish roots as a religion—to rejecting those roots by teaching contempt—to returning and seeing the value of our Jewish roots and Judaism itself? What has brought us full circle? THE HOLOCAUST! The Holocaust has become a catalyst for every human being, human institution, religion and race in Western civilization to reevaluate itself with prophetic self-criticism. The Holocaust has become the cornerstone for building a new society and world in which equal and civil rights are the governing clichés. The Holocaust has created a paradigm shift away from ghettos, alienation, and isolation to a world of global awareness, dialogue, and openness to diversity.

And so, where do we go from here? Keeping in mind the saying of St. Augustine, "We Christians are an Easter people," we must rise out of the ashes of Auschwitz and commit ourselves to the Easter gift of the risen Christ, who breathed a *new* life into his disciples with an *old* Jewish word, "Shalom," "Peace." Let each one of us who has been baptized into his resurrection open ourselves to that gift—become peace itself—and bring it on our lips, in our hearts, in our minds, in our very beings to everyone we meet!

Shalom Ha Mashiach (Peace of Christ be with you).
Sha'alu Shalom Shalayim (Pray for the peace of Jerusalem).
Shabbat Shalom (Sabbath peace)!

12.
HOLOCAUST: WEEK OF REMEMBRANCE

(Delivered at the annual Baltimore Jewish Council Day of Remembrance ceremony, April 30, 2006, at which I received the annual Greenblatt Award honoring those who remember the Holocaust)

Forty years ago, October 28, 1965, the Second Vatican Council of the Roman Catholic Church produced and promulgated a document that would change two thousand years of Christian persecution, Catholic teaching of contempt and religious anti-Semitism against the Jewish people.

In the flourish of new ideas and changes in the aftermath of the Council, this document entitled, "Nostra Aetate," went unnoticed by most of the Catholic world. I personally didn't know of it until its tenth anniversary celebrated in 1975.

"Nostra Aetate," which means in English, "In Our Time," set me, personally on the path that leads me here tonight. It was a milestone document that opened the door to dialogue between our two ancient communities: Roman Catholicism and Judaism. This document effected a change in attitude not only in me and my Church, but also has had a tremendous influence on how other religious groups have begun to view Judaism in a new light.

After thirty years of reflection and study of "Nostra Aetate," there is no doubt in my mind that the catalyst for this document and the Second Vatican Council itself was the tragedy and world-shattering event we now call "The Holocaust."

I was assigned to Towson (State) University in 1980 as campus minister. In my role as teacher, I began to teach the Bible from a

Jewish perspective—a scholarly approach that had developed worldwide in only the previous twenty-five years or so. In 1989, one of my Bible students, who was also a history major at TU and a collector of historical artifacts, encouraged and aided me in inaugurating an Annual Week of Remembrance at the Newman Center—home of the Catholic Campus Ministry at Towson University.

For seventeen years now, we have engaged in this Annual Week of Remembrance which has sparked a great deal of interreligious dialogue between the Catholic Newman Center and all facets of Jewish life here in Baltimore—rabbis, Holocaust survivors, Jewish faculty and students at TU, The Baltimore Jewish Council, Beth Torah Synagogue in Hyattsville, the Institute for Christian and Jewish Studies, and many more.

This endeavor led me to Israel twelve times, spending two summers studying the Holocaust at Yad Va Shem, the International Center for Holocaust Studies in Jerusalem.

All of this brings me to why I am here before you tonight—to humbly accept this award in the names of all those in the Newman Center Community and especially our Cardinal Newman Council of the Knights of Columbus, who have sponsored our Annual Week of Remembrance for the past ten years.

My own journey to this point has been gradual, focused, and life-giving. I have come to learn the value of the words of the Baal Shem Tov:
"Remembrance is Salvation
Forgetfulness is Exile."

When asked why a Catholic group would be interested in the Holocaust, I always give the following five reasons and I leave you with these final thoughts:

1. To be in solidarity with our brother and sister Jews by remembering with them their inestimable loss.
2. To educate the non-Jewish population about the need to understand what happened in this tragic crisis that affects all humanity.

3. To give Christians (and particularly Catholics) a sense of the Church's complicity in this gross action, as well as stories of the many righteous Gentiles who saved Jews at the peril of their own lives.

4. To demonstrate the universality of this horror and how it went beyond the Jewish community, as well as its uniqueness to the Jewish people themselves.

5. To prevent it from ever happening again by being witnesses to the survivors in hopes of counteracting revisionist history.

"Remembrance is Salvation while
Forgetfulness is Exile."
(Baal Shem Tov)

Thank **you** for **remembering** those of **us** who **remember!**

13.
INTERFAITH MARRIAGES

(Given at a workshop entitled "Nostra Aetate and Beyond" at St. Mary's Seminary, Baltimore, Maryland in 1991 for Jewish and Christian Clergy)

Good morning, everyone!

M y part of today's presentation will come in four parts:
Part I: An introduction of myself and my connection to today's topic, as well as the topic's connection to "Nostra Aetate."

Part II: The Roman Catholic Church's position on interfaith marriages on both universal and local levels.

Part III: My role as pastor in working with interfaith couples.

Part IV: Some questions and reflections for all of us to come to grips with.

PART I
Introduction

My name is Bob Albright and I am a Roman Catholic Priest of the Archdiocese of Baltimore. As a pastor in parochial work, I have been involved with interfaith couples since 1971 and in my present ministry as a University Campus Minister for the past thirteen years. Perhaps I bring a great deal of experience to this topic, but I certainly do not bring you answers to the issues involved. Historically, since the time of Vatican II and the writing of the document "Nostra Aetate," there has been an increase in ecumenical, as well as interfaith marriages. "Nostra Aetate" (and other Vatican II documents) opened doorways that had been shut for centuries. As each doorway was opened, another door lay ahead inviting and even tempting us to open it also. After centuries of isolation, hostility and competition, at least, the Roman Catholic Church, in the historic document we celebrate these two days, opened the door to dialogue between herself (and perhaps all Christians) and the Jewish people of our age. On the level of the ordinary Jew and the ordinary Catholic, this dialogue has resulted in numerous and increasing numbers of marriages between Jews and Catholics over the past twenty-five years.

PART II
The Roman Catholic Church's Position on Interfaith Marriages both on the Universal and Local Levels

The Church's position is clear, traditional, and obvious: she prefers that Catholics marry Catholics. The Church, however, is realistic and recognizes that the requests are increasing for interfaith marriages. To quote from the Pastoral Handbook of our own Archdiocese, you will see the care and sensitivity with which the Church goes about this ministry: "The priest or deacon who is helping a Catholic and a Jew to enter into marriage should be sensitive to the religious convictions and customs of both parties" (page 77, paragraph b). "Jewish rabbis are often not inclined to participate in the celebration of a marriage between one of their people and a Christian. This reluctance is based on theological considerations and deeply cherished religious convictions and should in no way be construed as ill will or an anti-Christian bias" (page 77, paragraph c).

Let me now quickly outline for you what our Catholic Church policy is regarding interfaith marriages. When a Catholic marrying a Jew wishes the Church to recognize the marriage:

1. The Jewish party need not convert to Catholicism in order to marry a Catholic and have that marriage recognized by the Church.
2. No pressure is even (or should be) put on the Jewish party to convert.
3. The Catholic party is given permission by the Church to have a Jewish ceremony (if desired) not in a church building or synagogue.
4. The Catholic Church recognizes the Jewish ceremony as valid in her eyes.
5. The priest may (but need not for validity) take part in the Jewish ceremony at the discretion of the rabbi and the couple.

6. A Catholic and Jew may be married in a Catholic ceremony (if desired) with the rabbi taking an active part.

Conditions placed on the couple themselves are as follows:

A. They need to attend premarital sessions with a priest or through diocesan programs.

B. The official papers of the Catholic Church must be filled out.

C. The interfaith marriage is recognized under one condition placed on the Catholic party to have the children baptized and raised Catholic.

PART III
My Role as Pastor, Counseling an Interfaith Couple

A. My own understanding of all the elements involved comes first. The covenantal nature of this sacred act and how that is played out from four perspectives:

1. Catholic Church—sees marriage as Sacramental.
2. Judaism—sees marriage as Identity.
3. The couple—sees marriage as Love.
4. The families—see marriage as Relationship.

All four perspectives are communities that view marriage as a perpetuation of that community. Belonging to God—belonging to a community—belonging to another human being—belonging to a people, a race, a religion—belonging is salvation. Everyone wants to BELONG, to be a part of something, someone. No one wants to be lost or alienated or forgotten. Belonging is Sacramental, is Identity, is Love, is Relationship. The problems arise when we want to belong to more than one community or family. The problems grow heavier when these communities or families differ in essence. The problems may be even insurmountable if these communities or families are diametrically opposed to one another (at least in practice and at this moment in history).

B. Care and sensitivity to all of the above becomes the central pastoral role. As a pastor, my role, then, becomes one of making the Jew a better Jew and the Catholic a better Catholic. My role is not to convert you to another religion, but strengthen your own. Coming to grips with one's own identity and each other's identity is the essential starting point. As pastor, my role is neither to talk an interfaith couple into marriage, nor out of it. My ministry must extend beyond the couple to the families and all who may be involved. There is a great need for openness and flexibility on my part *before* the wedding day and the need for support and guidance on my part *beyond* the wedding day.

C. Some issues encountered:

Re: Couples—I remember some coming to grips with each other's identity enough to talk themselves out of the marriage. I remember Jews who learned more about Judaism in preparing for marriage than they ever learned at home or in shul and Catholics who came to grips with being Catholic for the first time in their lives while preparing for an interfaith marriage.

Re: Families—At one wedding ceremony (a Jewish one in which I was participating) the Catholic father of the Catholic bride was not going to attend the ceremony if I didn't say the name of "Jesus" and the Jewish mother of the Jewish groom was not going to attend if I did!!!

PART IV
Some Questions and Reflections to Leave You with to Ponder
Not to Necessarily Solve Today at this Session

1. Are the differences between being a Jew and being a Christian any more insurmountable in an interfaith marriage than overcoming the differences in being a man or being a woman in any marriage?

2. Does the church and/or synagogue run the risk of losing many of its members by permitting interfaith marriages?

3. Does the church and/or synagogue run the risk of losing many of its members by <u>not</u> permitting interfaith marriages?

4. Since religion holds a monopoly over the sacred act of marriage in our world today, is it not necessary for the churches, mosques, and synagogues to be more flexible regarding interfaith marriages so as not run the risk of being accused of exercising undue control over people's lives?

5. Are Judaism and Christianity so diametrically opposed to one another in essence that an interfaith marriage can never work out?

6. Is marriage cultural or religious? Neither or both?

7. Is marriage an institution to perpetuate a certain set of beliefs, or a certain race, or a certain religion—or to perpetuate the human race?

14.
SERMON AT A JEWISH/CATHOLIC WEDDING

P lease permit me (a Gentile and a Christian) to adapt an old Jewish custom to today's celebration—the traditional four questions asked by the youngest child at every Seder meal.

It goes something like this (and, remember, this is an adaptation):
Why is this day different from all other days of the year?
On all other days of the year Jews and Gentiles go their own ways.
On all other days of the year Jews and Christians never pray together.
On all other days of the year Jews and Catholics rarely ever meet in the same place.

WHY IS THIS DAY DIFFERENT FROM ALL OTHER DAYS OF THE YEAR? Because we gather in this place and behold the covenant between a bride and groom...Because both Jew and Gentile gather in this same place...

On this day, two people, two traditions, two cultures, two histories are made one...Because on this day, we conceive of a world where children will not be hated because they are Jew or Gentile, because they will be both!

WHY IS THIS DAY DIFFERENT FROM ALL OTHER DAYS OF THE YEAR? Because on this day, the skeptics are reminded that Jesus was a Jew...

On this day, both traditions are reminded that Ruth was a Gentile who married Boaz, a Jew, and they were the great grandparents of King David...

On this day, we are reminded that Abraham and Sarah are the parents of all nations...

WHY IS THIS DAY DIFFERENT FROM ALL OTHER DAYS OF THE YEAR?

On this day, we celebrate a Catholic woman and a Jewish man entering a covenant of love, a symbol of their covenant with the one God, which _____ entered at birth, and _____ entered at baptism...

Today, we celebrate two people who have faced the real struggles of their diversity, yet want to pass this on to their children...

WHY IS THIS DAY DIFFERENT FROM ALL OTHER DAYS OF THE YEAR? Because after centuries of stained and spotted hands— this day, Jew and Gentile will use their hands to fondle and caress...

Because after centuries of sacking and burning each other's temples and churches—this day, we meet in a church to gather and to give...

Because after centuries of isolation and alienation—this day, we have been brought together to pray, to forgive and to begin a new life...

_____and_____, we thank **you** for making this day **different** from all other days of the year!

15.
HOMILY AT A JEWISH/CATHOLIC WEDDING

Readings: Song of Songs 2:8-10,14, 16a; 8:6-7a I Corinthians 12:31-13:8a

The longing of a bride for her groom…the longing of Israel for God…the longing of one person for another…the need to belong to someone…

To belong to someone is to enter a covenant: "I belong to you—you belong to me!" To belong to someone is to be saved: "We are one."

In the Song of Songs from the Hebrew Scriptures, verses of which we just heard read, that longing to belong is played out in the voices of two people. They could be any two people—like _____and_____—but certainly they are the voices of Israel and God, the human and the divine searching to belong to one another as a bride and groom, engaged in a love affair, betrothed as one, wedded in a covenant. In fact, it was Israel's covenant with God that taught Israel how to engage in human-to-human relationships.

In the Letter to the Corinthians from the Christian Scriptures, our second reading today, the Jewish apostle to the Gentiles—Paul—sets up the criteria for any covenant. The criterion for all covenants, all relationships, all marriages, is love. But did you notice that Paul's concept of love does not contain the usual romantic, emotional, or sexual nuances we often give to that word? This Scripture speaks of love as a gift, a mystery, and eternal—without end. Romance dies. Emotions are fleeting. Sexuality is cyclical. Love, if it is genuine, does not come to an end. Love goes beyond faith and trust and even beyond the one and only condition found in every marriage vow—until death—for love goes beyond death. Like the wedding ring—love is a circle without end.

Every marriage, then, between a Jew and a Christian is a reenactment of the covenant God made with the Jews through Moses and also with the Gentiles through Jesus. This covenant was and remains a covenant of mutual faith, trust, and love pledged forever.

_____and_____, as you come forward to make this pledge to one another, know what you are doing; know what you are saying. You symbolize that covenant made by God with both Jews and Christians. You also strengthen that covenant here in our midst in 1999 and 5760. And you belong to that covenant more deeply than ever, because you belong to one another!

16.
HOMILY AT A CATHOLIC/ PROTESTANT WEDDING

Readings: Genesis 2:18-24 I John 4:7-12 John 17:20-23

The theme of **Unity** runs through the Scripture _____ and ____ ____ have chosen for us to hear today. "And they became one"— the man and his wife (Genesis). "May they all be one"—the early Christian Church (John's Gospel). "God's love will be complete in us"— the believer who loves is one with God (John's Letter). The Scripture is telling us that **Unity** is the will of God. _____ and _____ are telling us that **Unity** is their plight, their goal, the hope for their relationship.

The Scripture also tells us that love and diversity are also God's will. The reason is that one cannot have unity without love and diversity. When diversity becomes a source of love, then there will be unity. When diversity becomes a source of discord, then there will be disunity or division. Unity is founded on love—not discord!

Since the beginning of the Church, there has been diversity within the Christian community, which sometimes led to love and other times to discord. It was discord that was the basis for Jesus' prayer that "all be one." It was discord that prompted the author of John's letter to write that the true Christian must be a lover, for love is of God (not discord). The author is even stronger when he says, "God is love!"

Since the beginning of the world, there has been diversity in creation that sometimes led to love and other times to discord. It must have been discord that reminded the author of Genesis to remind his listeners of the ideal of marriage—that husband and wife are one in the image of God—for God is one! Like all people since the beginning of creation and

Christianity, _____and_____ bring diversity to their relationship, their marriage. They bring the diversity of man and woman and all that that entails. They bring the diversity of Baptist and Catholic and all that that entails. What they do with this diversity will determine their life and the lives of their children.

If their diversity leads to love—there will be unity. If their diversity leads to discord—there will be division.

Diversity leads to discord: when people absolutize their diversity as right and another's as wrong; when people remain close-minded and want everything their way; when people treat diversity rather than similarity as essential. Diversity leads to love: when people see diversity as different rather than right or wrong; when people remain open to the diversity of life and see it as good; when diversity is seen as the only path to unity—for how can there even be unity without diversity?

_____and_____, so far you have done well—you have accepted and respected each other's diversity, each other's tradition—you are on the road to unity. May I offer one final piece of advice as you embark on your life's journey today: always keep your sights on Jesus as the source of unity in your Christian diversity and you will remain in love; always keep your sights on God as the source of unity in your human diversity and you will remain as one. For remember, the very Scripture you have chosen says: God is love. God is one.

In a moment, in a sacred moment, in a sacrament—you will join with the Father, and the Son, and the Holy Spirit in this awesome mystery called UNITY!

17.
HOMILY AT A BUDDHIST/CATHOLIC WEDDING

(This homily was given as a way to acquaint the Buddhist bride with the entire Jewish and Christian tradition of the groom, because this couple was going to go to Thailand where they would celebrate the wedding in the Buddhist tradition, as well)

Readings: Genesis 24:48-51, 58-67 I Corinthians 12:31-13:8a John 15:12-16

There are two great lessons we learn from the Hebrew Scripture that are appropriate for today's celebration.

Abraham lived in a world of polytheism, or belief in many gods. The world that surrounded Abraham and his household was one in which human destiny was determined by the gods and human fate was written in the stars. It was a world where no one had anything to say about his or her life. People were just pawns for the gods as they played the game of life. Nothing a person could do or say could sway the gods or change the stars.

In the midst of this gloomy and dooming existence, Abraham hears the voice of the one God and follows that voice immediately without question. The voice of that one God eventually leads Abraham to see that he has a free will and life is not predestined. Abraham learns (and we do too) the *first great lesson* taught in the Old Testament—"I" have something to say about my own life. "I" can play a significant role in my own destiny. "I" have a free will. "I" have been given the gift of choice.

The God of Abraham is a God who gives humans the freedom to make choices and decisions that will affect not only the one making the choice, but will affect other people as well. The God of Abraham is a God of freedom who allows Abraham to choose whether he will follow God or not. Abraham chooses to follow the one God and the two of them (God and Abraham) begin the greatest love affair the world has ever known.

God initiates a covenant with Abraham—a living, loving relationship—whereby Abraham and all his descendents will belong to God and God to them. The one God now becomes the God of Abraham, the God of Isaac (Abraham's son), and the God of Jacob (Isaac's son), and eventually the God of Israel. And thus, the *second great lesson* of the Old Testament begins to unfold. We heard part of that great story in our first reading from the Book of Genesis.

Marital relationships in the Bible come across as very sterile and utilitarian. Whether between Abraham and Sarah or Isaac and Rebecca or Jacob and Rachel, a marriage relationship was seen as a necessity to produce descendants who became a security, a workforce, a tribe, and carry on one's name after death. Many patriarchs and kings in the Old Testament had many wives for these very reasons. Marriage was a necessity, utilitarian, and rarely was the result of love and true relationship.

It was, on the other hand, the relationship between God and the people of Israel—the covenant—that becomes the second great lesson of the Hebrew Bible. In and through the covenant, God slowly taught Israel the purpose of a marriage relationship or any relationship. God taught Israel how to love, to remain faithful, to forgive, to be patient and kind, never jealous, boastful, or rude, not to take offense or be resentful or selfish, but to trust, hope, excuse, and endure whatever comes.

In the New Testament part of the Bible (the Christian Scripture) this lesson is expressed in Paul's Letter to the Corinthians when he writes: "If I have faith in all its fullness...but without love, then I am nothing at all."

And so, the two great lessons we learn today are: First, each human being has the freedom to choose and contribute to his/her own destiny; and second, that choosing the right relationships for the right reasons will help fulfill that destiny.

What wonderful lessons to be expressed in a wedding ceremony as two people begin a lifetime relationship.

The promises made between Israel and God in their covenant are no different than the ones made between a bride and groom in marriage, whether they be Jewish or Gentile.

For it was through the life, death and resurrection of Jesus, a descendent of Abraham, that we Gentiles (non-Jews) are able to enter that same covenant that God established with Abraham. And so, the promise made to Abraham by God that, in him, all the nations of the earth would be blessed, was fulfilled in Jesus of Nazareth and extended to the whole world through the Christian Church.

The God of the Bible is a God of the covenant—a God who takes pains to create new relationships—who takes pains to uncover lost relationships—who takes pains to renew broken relationships.

In the Letter to the Corinthians from the Christian Scriptures, the Jewish apostle to the Gentiles—Paul—sets up the criteria for any covenant. The criterion for all covenants, all relationships, all marriages, is love. But did you notice that Paul's concept of love does not contain the usual romantic, emotional, or sexual nuances we often give to that word. This Scripture speaks of love as a gift, a mystery, and eternal—without end. Romance dies. Emotions are fleeting. Sexuality is cyclical. Love, if it is genuine, does not come to an end. Love goes beyond faith and trust and even beyond the one and only condition found in every marriage vow— until death—for love goes beyond death. Like the wedding ring—love is a circle without end. It is this kind of love that Jesus speaks about in the Gospel of John—a love through which I can relate to God, another human, and myself.

Everyone wants a relationship—to belong, to be a part of something, someone. No one wants to be lost or alienated or forgotten. Belonging to God—belonging to a community—belonging to another human being—belonging to a people, a race, a religion, a family, an other... For the Jews, belonging gives identity. For the Christian, belonging is sacramental. For both, Jew and Christian, belonging is salvation!

Therefore, the message of all these words to us today is that relationships can be encounters with God! Every relationship is a potential encounter with God. Every relationship that has God at its center is covenantal.

To actualize that encounter, we must possess simple, ordinary faith like Abraham. St. Paul, in his Letter to the Corinthians, says it best, "Strive eagerly for the greater gifts." We must go beyond the facts, the physical, the ordinary, the so-called "self-evident." We must transcend our very selves—leave ourselves, go out of ourselves and leave our mother and father—take the risk to reach beyond ourselves to the other—meet the other where they are—love the other—let go of the other—return to ourselves, and recognize that somewhere between you and the other, there is God! This is the journey found in the Gospel: From love of self, to love of another, to love of God.

_____and_____ are doing that today. They have taken a new step in the journey of life—which is to discover God. They have chosen the relationship of marriage as their means of accomplishing this dream. They have chosen each other as the medium for discovering God.

And so _____and_____, today you are entering a mystery that reaches back to the beginning of time and forward into the future, beyond death itself.

It is the mystery of covenant. Marriage is one way of entering this mystery, which opens for you a doorway into the past and future.

Today you join with all those married couples down through the ages who have pledged and lived out faithfully their pledge to be faithful to God, themselves, and one another.

In doing this, you have begun your future—a future guaranteed only by your own faithful commitment to the vows you are about to make in the presence of God, one another, and all of us you have invited to join you here today.

God Bless you both as you begin to live those vows in the sacrament, the covenant, we call marriage!

18.
GOOD FRIDAY REFLECTIONS

(A Catholic Priest trying to speak authentically about a Jew of the New Testament to a Protestant Congregation of Christians in Trinity Episcopal Church, Towson, Maryland, 1991. Our task was to choose a minor character in the story from the passage we were given.)

Reading: Luke 22:63-71

I am a *Jew*—you know us—we believe in the one God!

I am a *Sadducee*—you've heard of us—we don't believe in the resurrection from the dead!

I am a *Chief Priest*—I am appointed by the governor, Pontius Pilate.

My name is *Asher*—and I live here with my family in Jerusalem.

The entire Sanhedrin is here today trying to keep the peace during the Passover. I am a member of this august body, whose duty it is to squelch any uprisings or subdue any undesirables like this guy, Yeshua, from Galilee. Last week he caused a stir at the gate of the city and shortly after that went about the temple like a mad man ejecting everyone in sight. Pilate was quite angry about all this and asked us to put a stop to it. That's why we're here today, even though it is the first day of the Passover. The crowds of Jews in the city this week are so large that Pilate is in fear of a Zealot revolt. I hope not—I'll lose my position if that happens.

Well, back to this Yeshua from Nazareth...I'm glad the Pharisees aren't here today; there would be quite a theological debate between them and this Yeshua, who is claiming every title held sacred in Judaism. He's

REV. ROBERT E. ALBRIGHT

quite unusual...He answers questions like a *Prophet*...He admits to being the *Messiah*...He alludes to being the *Son of Man*...He does not deny the title *Son of God*...How can this be???

In our sacred tradition, these titles belong to three separate persons who will be sent by God to carry out God's holy plan for Israel. First, will come the *Prophet* of the end time. His mission will be to announce the coming of the last days and to call for repentance. Next, will come the *Messiah* whose mission it will be to restore the people of Israel to their proper place among all the nations of the earth. Finally, the *Son of Man* will come to usher in the Kingdom of God, the new world order. All three of these sacred figures will be called *Sons of God*, for they come to do God's will and not their own.

Now, you see how unusual it is that this Yeshua from Galilee should let himself be called by all four of these titles! He is a Jew—an observant one from all we can tell. He knows our tradition about these three servants from God. Why does he allow these sacred titles to be applied to himself?!

Well, these are *theological* issues. I'll leave those questions for the Pharisees. I'm a Sadducee and a Chief Priest. My issue with this Yeshua is a *political* one. He's a nuisance. The governor is displeased. My job is to do whatever it takes to please the governor. So, we'll take Yeshua to Pilate. Pilate will throw him in prison for a few days until the Passover is passed. And then, he'll be released and sent back to Galilee where he belongs with all his silly theology.

And then we'll be able to tell the people: "Go to Galilee and there you will see him!"

19.
ROME AND THE PAPACY

(This homily was delivered during the period of mourning following the death of Pope John Paul II)

Readings: Acts 2:14, 22-28 I Peter 1:17-21 Luke 24:13-35

The Lord has been raised! It is true! He has appeared to Simon!" Apparently this phrase was one of the earliest professions of faith in the Church of the New Testament. It appears in various forms in the letters of St. Paul and the Gospels. That Simon (Peter) was graced with a special revelation and experience of the Risen Christ was not only the faith of the early Church, but even became a saying, a colloquialism, a formula, a written or memorized maxim prayed by believers and taught to converts entering Christianity (such as Saul who became Paul).

Simon Peter is clearly designated by the New Testament writers as the leading character in the Christian story and becomes the leader among leaders in the early Church tradition. As in our first reading today from the Acts of the Apostles, Peter in particular is named and singled out whenever the twelve (or eleven) apostles are referred to. Peter in the New Testament is that disciple who becomes chosen by Jesus, leads his brother and sister disciples to the faith, and stands before Paul, Jerusalem, Jews, and Gentiles as the number one witness in Christianity.

And because there is a strong legend that Peter and Paul were martyred by Nero in Rome, both of them have been closely associated with the Church of Rome from the beginning of Christianity. These thoughts have been the foundation for the establishment of the papacy and its alignment with the Church of Rome.

REV. ROBERT E. ALBRIGHT

Another reason for the Church of Rome to become the leading Christian community in the Church's tradition is that as early as 60 CE Paul writes in his letter to the Romans that they (the Roman Church) are heralded throughout the world for their unrivaled faith, perhaps because so many Christians in Rome were martyred for their faith (Romans 1:8).

So, very early in the New Testament itself, the connection between Peter and Rome became so strong that in the centuries to follow Rome supersedes even Jerusalem as the mother Church of Christianity.

As the Christian Church moved more and more away from Judaism and into the Gentile world, and in the fourth century became the state religion for the Western world, the Church of Rome became the natural symbol for authority and the first among equals. And as the Church in the second and third centuries began to move away from leadership by a group of presbyter-bishops to governance by a single bishop, the bishop of Rome became the symbol for Church unity in matters that involved various countries and cultures throughout the Western world.

The papacy, as we know it today, is built upon these biblical notions and historical developments in the first three hundred years of the Church's life. There have been 262 popes since the time of Jesus and a complicated history of the papacy for the past two thousand years. The purpose of the papacy has been a mission to the whole Church, who very early became diverse among many cultures and peoples and was not exempt from tensions and even conflicts. The role of the bishop of Rome was to act as an overseer in conflicts and even to have the authority given by Jesus to Peter when, in the Gospel of Matthew, Jesus changes Simon's name and tells him: "You are Peter, and on this rock I will build my church, and the gates of Hades will not prevail against it. I will give you the keys to the kingdom of heaven, and whatever you bind on earth will be bound in heaven, and whatever you loose on earth will be loosed in heaven" (Matthew 16:18-20).

Even the tradition of the popes taking a new name comes from Matthew's Gospel and the whole biblical tradition of people who are called by God to lead a new life either taking or receiving a new name from

God: Abram becomes Abraham; Sarai becomes Sarah; Jacob becomes Israel; Saul becomes Paul; Simon becomes Peter; Jesus becomes Christ!

How coincidental it is, that on the Sunday after our pope's funeral and within the nine days (or novena) of traditional mourning for the Pope, we have three Scripture readings that all mention Peter: Acts, I Peter, and Luke!

In one way, it is proof or evidence that Peter's role in the New Testament and the pope's role in the Church are synonymous and authentic.

Having a pope—especially in this age of globalization and expansion—is a gift from God. One of the main challenges of the papacy is to judge all tasks in the light of the Gospel in order to avoid turning its own authority into some political power.

Through the pope—especially in a world of overpopulation and a multiplicity of religions and philosophies—the Church can remain one, holy, catholic, and apostolic.

With a pope—especially as we go beyond this planet to the stars— the Church can model the virtues of faith, hope, and love in unity!

In a pope—especially in a universe of new and conflicting values— we can keep our identity as frail humanity who dies and rises over and over again, living the life of the man from Nazareth who forgave sins, gave himself totally to others, became the least among people, and conquered death!

What I have given you is the vision, tradition, and history of the papacy as it has come down to us.

Let us pray that the Holy Spirit will guide the cardinals of our Church to choose a person who can model the vision, remain true to the tradition, and face the challenges of history.

20.
"RERUM NOVARUM"
May 15, 1891

(This homily was delivered October 13, 1991, on the 100th Anniversary of the writing of the encyclical "Rerum Novarum" by Pope Leo XIII, along with the encyclical "Centesimus Annus" by Pope John Paul II.)

Readings: Wisdom 7:7-11 Psalm 14 Hebrews 4:12-13 Mark 10:17-30

A New Year had just begun…It was the year 1878…Pope Pius IX had just died (Pope Pius IX was the pope who called Vatican Council I). As is usual in the case of the death of a pope—the world mourns; the pope is buried; the college of cardinals convenes in Rome; a new pope is elected.

In 1878, there were few cardinals and the Church had just gone through a turbulent history. To whom should the cardinals look for a new pope? Not many of the Italian cardinals were very eligible since there were so few, and many beyond the age for a vibrant pope. Only one thing to do—look for a transitional pope—one who would not live long, yet strengthen the college of cardinals with more gifted men who could lead the Church triumphantly into the twentieth century.

On February 20, 1878, on the third ballot, in the Sistine Chapel, sixty-one cardinals elected the sickly and aging Cardinal Gioacchino Pecci as the new pope. He was sixty-eight years old and had previously been the Archbishop of Perugia in Italy for thirty-two years. The strategy was clear—this aging and sickly pope would bring the college of cardinals up to snuff so as to breed a healthy and younger successor. The new pope took the name LEO and was the thirteenth pope in the history of the Church with that name—thus he was known as Pope Leo XIII.

Well, shortly after his election to the papacy, Leo XIII regained his health and reigned as pope for twenty-five years, dying at the age of ninety-three!

Thus, this white-haired pontiff did not pass quietly and quickly into the shadows of history as people predicted, but he carried the Church chronologically and intellectually into the twentieth century as God intended him to do.

During his pontificate, he encountered many "new things" that the Church and world had never dealt with before: The papacy was stripped of all political and temporal powers for the first time in its history; anticlerical governments were springing up all throughout Europe; Church/state relations were crumbling; the industrial revolution was in full stride; and modernism was creeping up on an old entrenched world of theology.

At the behest of our own Baltimore's James Cardinal Gibbons for a papal examination of the moral implications of relationships between capital and labor, Pope Leo XIII responded with the now famous encyclical "Rerum Novarum" in 1891.

Describing the conditions that led to this landmark encyclical, Pope John Paul II, in his newest encyclical commemorating "Rerum Novarum's" one hundredth anniversary, had this to say:

> Toward the end of the last century the Church found herself facing a historical process which had already been taking place for some time but which was by then reaching a critical point. The determining factor in this process was a combination of radical changes which had taken place in the political, economic and social fields, and in the areas of science and technology, to say nothing of the wide influence of the prevailing ideologies. In the sphere of politics the result of these changes was a new conception of society and of the state, and consequently of authority itself. A traditional society was passing away and another was beginning to be formed—one which brought the hope of new freedoms, but also the threat of new forms of injustice and servitude. In the sphere of economics, in which scientific discoveries and their practical application come

together, new structures for the production of consumer goods had progressively taken shape. A new form of property had appeared—capital; and a new form of labor—labor for wages, characterized by high rates of production which lacked due regard for sex, age or family situation and were determined solely by efficiency, with a view to increasing profits. In this way labor became a commodity to be freely bought and sold on the market, its price determined by the law of supply and demand without taking into account the bare minimum required for the support of the individual and his family. Moreover, the worker was not even sure of being able to sell "his own commodity," continually threatened as he was by unemployment, which in the absence of any kind of social security meant the specter of death by starvation ("Centesimus Annus," Ch.1, Para. 4).

Pope Leo moved right into this tangled web of circumstances with courage, background, and experience, as well as an astute intellect to produce an encyclical that marked a new approach to social thinking at a time when the Church needed a new approach to make an impact on society.

This milestone encyclical, "Rerum Novarum," the one hundredth anniversary of which we celebrate today, was Leo's way of not only addressing the needs of his day, but also giving the Church a new paradigm in which to operate for at least one hundred years. "Rerum Novarum," which means in Latin "New Things," dealt primarily with the conflict between capital and labor or—as the encyclical calls it—the worker question.

Pope Leo, in his encyclical, affirmed the rights of workers. The dignity of the worker and the dignity of work itself lay at the foundation of this document. In Leo's eyes, work belongs to the vocation of every person—indeed, people express and fulfill themselves by working. The encyclical devotes many pages to the question of private property and upholds the right of the individual to property. Another right called for in "Rerum Novarum" is the natural human right to form private associations or trade unions. This was a new idea in the nineteenth century, even though we take it for granted today. Along with this right, the encyclical stresses related rights which include limited working hours, the right to legitimate rest, and the right of children and women to be treated differently with regard to the type and duration of work. Just wages and the right to discharge freely one's religious duties are called for in "Rerum Novarum."

Leo criticized two social and economic systems—socialism and liberalism: socialism for its false ideology about the importance of work; liberalism for its favoring the rich over the poor. In his encyclical, Leo said: "When there is question of defending the rights of individuals, the defenseless and the poor have a claim to special consideration. The richer class has many ways of shielding itself and stands less in need of help from the state; whereas the mass of the poor have no resources of their own to fall back on and must chiefly depend on the assistance of the state. It is for this reason that wage earners, since they mostly belong to the latter class, should be specially cared for and protected by the government" ("Rerum Novarum" Parag. 125).

The greatest significance "Rerum Novarum" had for the Church was the model to "meddle" in world affairs. This encyclical was the first time the Church set out to critique the political, economic, and social structures of society. "Rerum Novarum" opened the doorway for future popes and generations to comment on their world, not just to criticize, but to offer concrete and realistic alternate pathways whereby all social beings could live in social justice. "Rerum Novarum" spawned social reforms that today we take for granted—such as the social security system, workers' compensation, and pension plans. A hundred years ago, these benefits were not even heard of.

The Catholic social teaching begun with "Rerum Novarum" has influenced much of what has been done in this country and all over the world for the past one hundred years. We stand on the shoulders of giants like Popes Leo XIII, Pius XI, Pius XII, John XXIII, Paul VI, and John Paul II who have charted the course of this past century with their examples and their social encyclicals; like Dorothy Day and Brendan Walsh of the Lay Catholic Worker movement; like St. Elizabeth Ann Seton and Mother Teresa of Calcutta and other religious men and women who bring justice to the needy; like James Cardinal Gibbons, Monsignor Ryan, and Monsignor Higgins and other activist priests and bishops in our country's history. The legacy of "Rerum Novarum" lives on—it is alive and well not only in the social *teaching*, but also the social *action* of the Roman Catholic Church in the United States and elsewhere.

However, there is much yet to be done before that "City of Peace" (spoken about in every social encyclical) will appear. People of conscience and justice must rise up in the midst of this world like Solomon choosing wisdom over scepter and throne. College students, unlike the rich young man in the Gospel, must begin to choose eternal life over the material riches of this world. More of us sitting here must get involved in social justice causes. Rather than being "no ones" who are apathetic, we must become "some ones" who will do and be justice. There are still those who ravage the earth and lay waste the land. They claim there is no God—there is no justice. They strut and pose denying all that we believe in. They strangle the poor and plunder society. The world is filled with people who have no morals, no shame, who squander and abuse people, devouring them as bread. These people bargain our very birthrights.

The Church's social teaching calls all of us—like Pope Leo—to take the risk and jump right into the middle of all this and cry, "I will be justice among you." The encyclicals of the past restore our faith in the often-forgotten "God of the Abandoned." Catholic social teaching calls for a transformation of the earth, a reforming of shattered dreams and a building up of the City of Peace here in this world—a city with safe homes of peace, children at play, flowers, light and melody—a city without death or darkness where the sun will someday be needed by us no more!

21.
JOHN HENRY NEWMAN

Any volume of sermons and homilies on the theme of ecumenism would have to include something about the giant thinker and prolific writer of the nineteenth century, John Henry Newman. To acquaint the reader with this outstanding figure in Church history one must also know something of the historical context of the time in which he lived.

Using the previous homily (number twenty) as a partial background, Newman lived at a very interesting moment in history. The eighteenth century was a time of revolutions: *the Enlightenment* (an educational revolution); *the Industrial Revolution* (a social revolution); *the French and American Revolutions* (political revolutions); *loss of the Papal States* (a religious revolution). It was a time that sparked anticlericalism in Europe, Church/ state tensions, and produced a society of rational thinking that reasoned God out of existence.

Newman's own nineteenth century found him alongside great figures such as Charles Darwin, William Wadsworth Longfellow, Karl Marx, Beethoven, and Pasteur, to name a few. It was a time of giant scholars and thinkers, along with many activists who have influenced the world even to the present day.

Below in simple outline, I will give you a summary of the life of John Henry Newman, along with many of his accomplishments. Then I shall follow that by a few words of commentary on his life and influence so that you may see how crucial he has been to the development of theology, philosophy, education, and spirituality.

John Henry Newman

1801-06   +Is born February 21st in London, England to
John Newman (a banker) and Jemima Fourdrinier. Oldest of

six children (1802 Charles Robert, 1803 Harriet, 1805 Francis, 1807 Jemima, 1809 Mary Sophia). At an early age, John Henry has a profound admiration of Shakespeare and a passionate love of music.

1807-16   +Receives private schooling at Ealing School where he masters Greek and Latin, learns to play the violin and writes Spy and Anti-Spy (two newspapers that contradicted each other on issues). Writer of riddles. Wanders from his Anglican upbringing and religion in general.

1816-20   +Attends Trinity College at Oxford where he is elected scholar and receives BA degree. Converts back to the Church of England and decides to remain single and devotes his life entirely to God.

1822-23   +Becomes a Fellow at Oriel College in Oxford where he receives his MA degree.

1824   +Is ordained deacon for the Church of England and becomes the curate of St. Clement's while retaining his Fellowship at Oriel. His father dies that summer.

1825   +Is ordained priest for the Church of England. Appointed vice principal, bursar, and chaplain of Alban Hall at Oriel.

1828   +Is appointed vicar of the University Church of St. Mary the Virgin at Oxford.

1832   +Forms notable friendships with Hurrell Froude, John Keble, Edward Pusey. After resigning his Oriel tutorship, takes a Mediterranean tour on which he writes "Lead Kindly Light," a still famous text sung in Christian churches today.

1833-41   +"The Oxford Movement" is started by Newman along with Keble, Froude, and Pusey. They wrote tracts and had them published and they distribute them personally in an attempt to renew the spiritual and intellectual life of the church and university in England. Many journey from all over England to hear Newman preach at Oxford. His mother dies in 1836.

1842   +At Littlemore, outside Oxford, Newman forms a small religious community that includes a new friend named Ambrose St. John who joined the Roman Catholic Church before Newman and was Newman's secretary and lifelong friend. In quasi-seclusion Newman wrote *"An Essay on the Development of Christian Doctrine."* Newman begins to question his place in the Church of England.

1845   +Resigns his Oriel College Fellowship and is received into the Roman Catholic Church by Father Dominic Barberi, CP, on October 9th at Littlemore, as a result of which he loses the friendship of many in his family and close friends.

1847   +Is ordained a Catholic priest in Rome. Joins the Oratory of St. Philip Neri and returns home to start an English Oratory in Birmingham.

1848-50   +Writes Loss and Gain (a novel about conversion). Pope Pius IX awards doctor of divinity to Father John Henry Newman.

1851   +Writes "The Present Position of Catholics." Achilli, a defrocked Dominican and convert to Protestantism exposed by Newman as a slanderer against Catholicism and a sex offender, is put on trial (a painful time for Father Newman).

1851-58   +Is sent as rector and founder of the Catholic University in Ireland, later University College, Dublin. Writes discourses on the scope and nature of university education addressed to the Catholics of Dublin, later collected into the book The Idea of a University.

1859   +Returns to England and starts a boarding school for about seventy boys next to the Oratory and appoints Father Ambrose St. John its headmaster.

1864-66   +Is attacked publicly by author Charles Kingsley, Newman responds with "Apologia pro Vita Sua." He writes "The Dream of Gerontius" and "Verses on Various Occasions."

1866   +Newman receives Gerard Manley Hopkins into the Roman Catholic Church and eventually leads him to becoming a Jesuit.

1867   +Denied permission to establish an Oratory at Oxford. Opposes erroneous definitions of Papal Infallibility by the Ultramontanes.

1870   +Writes "An Essay in Aid of a Grammar of Assent" (on the nature of religious belief).

1875   +Ambrose St. John dies and is buried outside Birmingham at the Oratory retreat of Rednal. This is a painful loss for Father Newman.

1877   +Is elected first honorary Fellow of Trinity College, Oxford.

1879   +Is created cardinal of the Church by Pope Leo XIII on May 12th.

1890   +Dies August 11th and buried in the same grave with Ambrose St. John at Rednal. On his gravestone it says: Ex umbris et imaginibus in veritatem (Out of the shadows and images into the truth).

Newman was a highly respected scholar and thinker in his day, as well as today. He was an extremely prolific writer. There are seventy thousand pages of his writings that were compiled as part of his canonization process. He was a profound preacher. People came from all over to hear him preach. Personally, he was a spiritual and holy man. He was a beloved teacher. Once when he was sick, the children in his class came to the Oratory and asked if Cardinal Newman could come out to play. He was prophetic in his views of the laity in the Church and in many of his writings sported a great sense of humor.

Newman appreciated nature and the mystery of the universe which can be seen in his writing of *"The Second Spring."* His contributions to the world of higher education are inestimable. His work *The Idea of a University* became the inspiration for ministry by the Catholic Church at colleges and universities throughout the world and especially in the United States where his name is used on centers and for student clubs and where his book is still used in college classrooms in both private and state schools alike.

John Henry Cardinal Newman was a man of faith and a lifelong pilgrim in search of the truth. Since the writing of this original sermon, he has been beatified toward canonization as a saint in the Roman Catholic Church. In both the Anglican and Roman traditions of Christianity as well as among countless other religious traditions, Newman's work and life are models for the "**Ecumenical Christian.**"

22.
THE ROLE OF THE LAITY IN THE CHURCH

(Delivered at the installation of a student peer minister for the campus ministry staff at Towson State University in Maryland on September 17, 2000.)

Readings: Sirach 27:30-28:9 Romans 14:7-9 Matthew 18:21-35

When one looks over the vast two-thousand-year history of the Christian Roman Catholic Church, one will find very little activity in the Church being ascribed to laymen and laywomen. The past two thousand years of Church history have been traditionally filled with the lives and activities of popes, bishops, monks, priests, nuns, abbots and abbesses, a king or queen here and there, and even fewer laymen or laywomen, let alone children. For most of Western civilization and the Church's role in it, the clergy and religious have had the spotlight, and for all intent and purposes usurped the rights of the baptized. While this all looks bad, there is a reasonable explanation for this—for most of our history in the Western world, we have been basically an illiterate people. In the past and especially through the so-called "medieval ages" only clergy and nobility were educated. The historical quip made by the "king" to the "bishop" was: "You keep them stupid and I'll keep them poor." With such a lock and monopoly on the culture, the ordinary person remained in the dark closet of history.

In light of all this, there are some other very interesting historical facts about Christianity that don't seem to fit into this pattern of history—and I refer especially to the first three hundred years of Christianity. Jesus was a layman. He was not a rabbi or a high priest. The twelve apostles and the women who surrounded Jesus were poor and uneducated laymen and laywomen. In fact, many scholars today would posit that Jesus probably could not read or write. He was a verbal storyteller of parables. We don't have one solitary word written by Jesus or any of his disciples in the New

Testament. The New Testament was written by well-educated Jews and Hellenists such as Paul, Mark, Matthew, Luke, and John—all in the latter part of the first century, long after Jesus and the apostles were dead.

Somehow, then, this history of the New Testament doesn't jibe with the rest of our history as a Church. Our founding fathers and mothers were laypeople, uneducated and poor. Our medieval fathers and mothers were clergy and nobility who were rich and well-educated and who therefore naturally usurped the rights and role of the ordinary baptized laymen and laywomen.

Piercing through this paradoxical history always comes a voice from God, a messenger of Good News, someone so close to God that the only words spoken are God's. Right in the middle of cultural upheaval, political revolution, social modernism, and educational enlightenment of the nineteenth century comes a voice that says:

I want an intelligent, well-instructed laity. I wish you to enlarge your knowledge, to cultivate your reason, to understand how faith and reason stand in relation to each other, and what are the bases and principles of Catholicism.

These are the words of John Henry Cardinal Newman who lived between 1801 and 1890. Listen how he balances out our Christian history in these words. He says: "I want the intellectual layman to be religious, and the devout ecclesiastic to be intellectual."

Cardinal Newman was the greatest champion of the layperson in our Church and he prophetically spoke these words on behalf of all those who have been and are oppressed by clericalism and elitism everywhere. He said: "The voice of the **whole** Church will, in time, make itself heard."

For John Henry Newman, that would be the voice of God, when "The whole Church" could speak openly and without oppression. In the 1860s—one hundred years before Vatican II—Newman wrote an *"Essay on Consulting the Faithful in Matters of Doctrine."* Some bishops in England and Rome thought Newman's ideas about the role of laity in the Church were heretical. In defiance of this essay, one bishop wrote to Newman and in his letter defiantly asks: "Who are the laity anyway?" Newman wrote back in reply: "Without the laity, bishop, the Church would look foolish."

In 1960, another man named "John," Pope John XXIII heard this same voice of God and wanted to proclaim it in the universal Church and so he called the Second Vatican Council (1962-65). Vatican II took up the cause of all the baptized in such documents as "The Declaration on Religious Freedom," "Decree on the Apostolate of the Laity," "Declaration on Christian Education," and in *"Lumen Gentium,"* one of the greatest documents in our Church history, "The Constitution on the Church," which states:

> The laity...are by baptism made one body with Christ and are constituted among the People of God; they are in their own way made sharers in the priestly, prophetical and kingly function of Christ; and they carry out for their own part the mission of the whole Christian people in the Church and in the world. (#31)

All of what I have just very briefly demonstrated are the bases for our program of peer ministry here at the center named after John Henry Cardinal Newman. Our program, which began in 1985 and today sees the installation of its fourteenth peer minister, is one that takes seriously our history and the voice of God in that history. It is a program that hands the real ministry of the Church over to laymen and laywomen—a ministry that is their right by baptism and not ordination. Our peer ministers are not nuns or clerics. Nor are they necessarily persons preparing for priesthood or the convent. They are and remain laymen and laywomen, students of Towson State University and the Catholic Church who are willing to minister to their fellow students.

In our brochure is a detailed description of how we choose peer ministers and what their duties entail. My intention in this sermon would show you the historical and theological context out of which this ministry originates. And, as you will note in reading our brochure, the Ministry to Higher Education becomes an ideal setting in which to exercise this type of ministry—for every institution of higher learning boasts of training, educating, and enabling future leaders. We, here at this Newman Center and Newman Centers all over the world, join the world of higher education in this great opportunity of forming future leaders for society and the Church.

Today, we celebrate not only the peer ministry itself, but the installation of our fourteenth peer minister, _____. He enters a world prepared for by the greatest minds and spirits in our history—Pope John XXIII, John Henry Cardinal Newman, and Jesus, himself, the *layperson* par excellence who ministered to his peers so faithfully that God raised up the Church to continue his work, in his name, to every nation, in every age, forever and ever. Amen!

23.
PRIESTHOOD OF THE LAITY

Readings: Numbers 11:25-29 Mark 9:38-43,45,47-48

There seems to be some tension and jealousy displayed in the readings above. The invested prophets of the Old Testament are threatened by those not of their number who are also engaged in prophecy. The twelve apostles in the New Testament are threatened by those who have not been chosen by Jesus and are casting out devils in his name. The institution or established structure becomes threatened when someone outside the institution or established structure performs the same service or function as one who is part of the institution or structure. But Jesus soothes the tension and explains: "One who is for us cannot be against us."

It is commonplace nowadays to say that all institutions are in crisis. This applies to secular as well as religious. People are beginning to question the very need of institutions as we know them today. The Church, in particular the Catholic Church, is a glaring example. Up until recently its institutional facade seemed impenetrable and fixed. The "system" or institution itself became sacralized. People simply had to adhere to its prudent laws and their consciences would be clear. It became an end in itself! And there are those who badly want it to return to those days again.

Since Vatican Council II, there has been an ongoing reform of the Church as an institution. We have seen reforms in such fundamental matters as liturgy and communications between central and outlying authorities. And in this process it is being disclosed how the need for reform actually goes much deeper than was thought. Let us look, for example, at the problem of the clergy vs. the laity—the institutional Church vs. the Church at large.

For centuries now, theologians, bishops, and popes have discussed the sacrament of ordination with great care only to bring to light a conflict or dilemma, which, until the present, has found no clarification. The question arises: are holy orders simply an *intensification* of that priesthood given at baptism or are holy orders a *different kind* of priesthood than the one given by baptism? In other words, are the clergy different from the laity?

I don't pretend to give an answer to this question, which has been considered by greater people than myself, but I would like to shed some light on this tension. Vatican II has made the following statement on priesthood: "In him (Jesus Christ) all the faithful are made a holy and royal priesthood; they offer spiritual sacrifices to God through Jesus Christ, and they proclaim the perfections of him who has called them out of darkness into his marvelous light. Therefore, there is no member who does not have a part in the mission of the whole body...The same Lord, however, has established ministers among his faithful to unite them together in one body in 'which not all the members have the same function'" (Romans 12:4). (*"Decree on the Ministry and Life of Priests"* Chapter 1, Parag. 2)

So it is then, by baptism, we are all called to priesthood, not ordination necessarily, but what some have called in recent years, *the priesthood of the laity*. All men and women who are baptized are called to a life of service and this service might sometimes be identical with that given by an ordained person, like myself.

Ordination does not reserve the right to serve, but it makes that right of baptism into a self-imposed, full-time lifestyle. This, however, does not exclude others who are not ordained from doing this also. It is not necessary to be ordained to visit someone in a hospital...It is not necessary to be ordained to distribute communion...It is not necessary to be ordained to lead a community in prayer...It is not necessary to be ordained to preach the Gospel...It is not necessary to be ordained to be the chancellor of a diocese or a pastoral life director.

St. Paul tells us that the Spirit works in many ways and for some it means to be a prophet, for others to be teachers, some apostles, some healers, and yet in all these cases one need not be ordained formally into the hierarchy, but rather ordained by the Spirit through baptism and confirmation. In St. Paul's lifetime, there was no hierarchy, nor clergy.

The Spirit is free to act independently of established structures. The Spirit is not exclusive—no one is ever refused. Why not communion in the hand? Why not women in the sanctuary? Why not married deacons? Why not lay ministers of communion? Why not laymen and laywomen preaching and reading the word of God? This is what we all have been called to do—to love and serve one another.

These people do not suffocate nor supplant the ordained minister—the established structure. Therefore, in this changing Church, the ordained deacon, priest, and bishop emerge not as an oppressed class of clergy, separate from the rest of the world, but rather a Spirit-filled leadership supported by all people, and nourished in the shared concern of every man and woman for his Church, his people, his body.

Jesus, himself, accepted all institutions with complete freedom, without ever letting himself become enslaved by them. He saw institutions and structures as servants of people. He restored them to their proper places, because they were made for people and not people for institutions. He saw them contributing to people's destiny and growth and, where this was not so through lack of service, he criticized and remodeled them, or, if necessary, abolished them, and he was a layperson, like yourselves. The Church, especially, must imitate the Spirit of Jesus and always be willing to criticize itself, for only in this way can it survive. And who is the Church? People—you and me—we are the Church! We must always be open as Jesus was and never exclude anyone. We must include all people in the role of ministers, not just those designated by the system. We must include every man and woman who desires to carry out the mission of Jesus..."For whoever is not against us is for us."

24.
THE INTELLECTUAL LIFE OF THE CHURCH

Never in the history of the world or the Church has there been such a surge in the intellectual life of people as there has been in our age. Since the invention of movable type by Johannes Gutenberg in 1440, volumes of books, journals, treatises, magazines, pamphlets, and the like have flourished beyond imagination. At this very moment in history, publishing and printing houses are innumerable; the amount of printed material is astounding. There are books ranging from junk to substance. TV, films, and radio have produced hundreds and thousands of educational specials on every subject imaginable. Schools and universities are overcrowded. Hospitals and research laboratories are studying round the clock to discover something new that will ease pain and suffering. People everywhere, in all walks of life are going back to school. Every man, woman, and child (it seems) is involved in developing their intellect, whether they want to or not.

The intellectual life of people is obviously on the rise. The human person is developing more and more today through education than ever before in history. And one of the most astounding discoveries made by education in recent times is that the human person is not only made up of diverse components, but must also strive to keep a balance among them. Every person is a little bit spiritual and a little bit bodily, a little bit emotional and a little bit intellectual. To live is to balance these components one with the other! To be overly spiritual can lead to neglect and fantasizing. To be overly bodily can make us vain and unapproachable. To be overly emotional can cause us to become morose or volatile. To be overly intellectual can make of us cold and rigid robots. It is this last component we wish to discuss in this sermon.

Forgive me for dissecting the human person in this way. We know, of course, that in reality a human being is an integrated person who balances and develops all components of self to perfection, never neglecting one for the other. Speaking about components of the human person is only a necessity so that we may better understand the topic we have chosen for this sermon...So here we go!

Our emotions tend to label something as right or wrong, but it is our intellect that helps us cope with right and wrong, and see beyond the labels we tend to use. Our emotions say that the Holocaust was wrong, but our intellect is able to discover a greater knowledge about people through this tragedy. Our emotions cringe from the turmoil and revolution in third world countries (and rightly so), yet our intellect discerns the motives for these actions and can find revolution a necessity at times. Our emotions blurt out what a great country this is in which we live, yet our intellect points to the exploitation, high taxation, militant fight for power, the arms race and other aspects of American life which prove the contrary. Our emotions can lead us off to foreign lands to preach the gospel or to build churches to evangelize, yet it is our intellect that makes known the risks and poses the questions we sometime try to cover over. Our emotions fill us with prejudice against other races and religions, but our intellect tells us they are no different than we. There are times, on the other hand, when our emotions are an asset and prevent us from harm or allow us to release our tension, but these are few and far between. Yet "His sun rises on the bad and the good, he rains on the just and the unjust" (Matthew 5:45).

Balancing these two components of our person is a lifetime process—a process to which the Church has always been and is committed to even today. The emotions are our natural reflexes and reactions (fear, anger, passion, etc.)—ones that come automatically with no effort. The intellect is that part of us that perceives and understands ideas through the thinking process. Both the intellect and emotions need discipline, but for different reasons. The emotions must be disciplined enough so as not to oppose the conscience in right decision making. The intellect must be disciplined to accept and perfect the knowledge and ideas that are transmitted to it by life. You can see why over the centuries saints and mystics have struggled for this perfection. It is in the perfect balance of these two (intellect and emotion) that the presence of God is most deeply experienced. "In a word, you must be perfected as your heavenly Father is perfect" (Matthew 5:48).

The intellectual life of the Church, then, is that component of the Church that accepts and perfects the knowledge and ideas it has about life, God, and people. It is that part of Church life that studies and ponders the mysteries of life. It is that portion of the Church that deals with the questions that life raises, which confronts the revelation we have inherited, and defines some plan for a future. This is the intellectual life of the Church: theology, philosophy, biology, Christology, sociology, ecclesiology, eschatology, logic, biblical studies, psychology, morality, and much more.

At the present time in the Church, the intellectual life of the Christian is available more and more to the layperson than in the past. In the past, only clerics and religious studied theology, philosophy, and the Bible. And, as a matter of fact, it was from those circumstances that the term "layperson" developed. The layperson is defined as the one *outside* the circle of those who are *in the know,* the one who doesn't know the jargon and inner workings of a particular group, the one who isn't "ordained" or commissioned or initiated. However, in today's Church that is changing, because in some cases the so-called layperson is more knowledgeable in theological matters than even bishops.

The intellectual life of the Church today belongs to every baptized Christian and not just to the clerics and theologians. Adult education courses have mushroomed all over the Church. Religious programs for public school students are organized in every parish. Prayer groups and small communities are gaining an ever-greater knowledge of theology, liturgy, and the Bible. Newman Centers of ministry and education are found at almost every secular college and university. The changes in the liturgy themselves have enhanced the preaching and education of every Church attendee. The "lay" man and woman are part of collegial bodies governing parishes, schools, and all areas of the Church's intellectual life. More and more laypeople are majoring in theology and teaching seminarians and students in Catholic colleges, universities, high schools, and seminaries. The intellectual life of the Church is no longer the sole responsibility of clerics and religious, but of all men and women called to the Church of Jesus Christ.

The hope for the future of the Church will be in its intellectual life. Every intellect strives to seek the truth. It is the truth that will make us free! Jesus defines truth as knowing God. He not only claims to speak the truth, but claims that he is the truth, the way, and the life. Ultimately, then, for the Christian, the truth is a person—Jesus Christ—God! Using one's intellect and coming to know the one true God is eternal life. Therefore, if our intellect is the means whereby we will acquire the truth, then it will also be the source of gaining everlasting life.

There can be no better reason for cherishing and nurturing the intellectual life in the Church. If we study, read, dialogue, listen, and take the risks involved in fully educating ourselves and others, we will be participating in the mystery of salvation. Education is liberation, and the theological term for liberation is salvation. It is for these reasons that the Catholic Church has set as its priority the intellectual development of its members. We have tried over the years to educate each other, to teach each other, to evangelize each other, to train each other in the art of dialogue. We have strived to break down the barriers of ignorance that have plagued us since childhood. We have attempted to dissolve the myths that hold us captive and keep us from reality. We have struggled to break through the prejudices that isolate us from one another. But...we have only begun. The intellectual process is a long and hard journey, complicated at times by our emotions, only to be dimmed for a moment in death.

Once again, we are the Church! The Church buildings will come and go, but we have a chance. We are not like buildings or bricks, or birds—we have an intellect, we can dream and think and know and labor and suffer and love and believe and hope. Our life has meaning, because we can seek the truth. The beauty of this search is that we can do it *together*. That means we can sing and dialogue and pray. We need not be silent...We need not be lost. We need not never know. But in the Church we can come to search and research about those things in life that have the deepest meaning for us. This is the only place I know of where we can do this! In the Church we can **be** someone, **know** someone, **believe with** someone, **believe in** someone, **love** someone, **speak with** someone, and **live, live, live!**

25.
ANNUAL CHRISTIAN UNITY OCTAVE

Most of us Catholics today can remember being told and taught as youngsters—that it was wrong to attend a Protestant church service or even enter a Protestant Church...We can also remember that when a Catholic married a Protestant it had to be done by the priest in a parlor of the rectory...(Maybe this is the case with some reading this?). We sadly remember the teaching that it was "Protestant" to have a Bible in your home and therefore most Catholics didn't have one at home, and some still don't. We also refused to admit to the validity of baptism in a Protestant church, so that if someone became a convert, they had to be "rebaptized."

It seemed for years that pettiness on both sides about uniformity kept us apart. Everyone was focused in on the things that divided us instead of the very one that united us. We (Protestants and Catholics) have always been united in **Jesus Christ**! Jesus is our redeemer—our example—our way. It was his final prayer the night before he died that we might all be united—not necessarily uniform—but united.

How far we have come in accomplishing our savior's last wish, just since our childhood to the present, is a sign that his Spirit is truly alive among us, guiding us and strengthening us in this important endeavor of unity among all people and not just Christians. How far have we come? Did you know that when a Catholic marries a Protestant today that it is not only done in a church, but in either the Protestant or the Catholic church—and that the priest can participate in the Protestant service or the minister in the Catholic service? This is true even for marriages between Catholics and Jews or the members of Orthodox faiths. I think you are aware of the ecumenical services held among all Christian churches. You've probably attended some yourselves. There also has been much dialogue between Protestant and Catholic theologians and hierarchies, as well as on the local level. In fact, I have spoken myself many times at Protestant churches on the Catholic liturgy and preached from their pulpits on Good Friday. The new prayers in the Mass (Gloria, Creed, Holy, Holy, etc.) are translations agreed upon by both Protestant and Catholic theologians. Baptism is no longer an obstacle, but recognized by our church even when done by a Protestant minister in a Protestant church. At most universities there are unions of ministers who are Catholic, Baptist, Lutheran, Episcopal, Methodist, Presbyterian, United Church of Christ, as well as other faiths. And the future holds the day when an agreed-upon translation of the Bible on the part of all Christian churches will be approved and printed. It is now being worked on!

One could say even that there is no longer an ecumenical problem, that the doors to unity have finally been open.

We cannot live with the mistakes our ancestors made—both Catholic and Protestant. We must be open to them and they to us! We must do all we can to understand them and they us! We cannot be so bold as to say one is wrong and one is right—we must, however, be willing to face all truths that we can work out together!

And this is why we must pray! And so we make our prayer with Jesus, but more than that we should live that prayer: "I pray that they may all be one, O Father! May they be in us, just as you are in me and I am in you. May they be one, so that the world will believe that you sent me" (John 17:21).

26.
CATHOLIC AND LUTHERAN CALL FOR UNITY

(This homily was given at the opening service of the Annual Lutheran Campus Ministers Conference in Collegeville, Minnesota, August 2, 1981, in which the Catholic Campus Ministers were invited to attend and participate.)

Readings: Isaiah 42:5-9 Matthew 5:13-16

> *Awake, you who sleep,*
> *Rise up from the dead,*
> *And Christ will be your Light!*

(This text of the Dutch poet and priest, Huub Oosterhuis, was sung as the opening song.)

Awake: from hundreds of years of slumber—almost four hundred years of tossing and turning, of restless nights, of closed eyes, of darkness and fears, of thinking "will this ever end?"

Awake, you who sleep: you have been asleep too long, hidden, under a bushel; asleep with prejudices, apathy, and division destroying your dreams; asleep with laws and offices and functions becoming your nightmares.

Awake, you who sleep, Rise up from the dead: the death of separation and endlessness, the death of hatred and apathy, the death of silence, misunderstanding, and mistrust.

Awake, you who sleep, Rise up from the dead, And Christ will be your Light: and now we are being called to awaken to the light, to something new, to the dawn, to the wisdom of a new day, to a voice that says, "Why stand staring at what has happened...once you were in the darkness, but now you are light...you are the salt of the earth...I am doing something new, haven't you noticed!"

Who is this voice? Who knows from whence it comes? Who sees when it arrives?

There have been people for whom this voice mattered above all else. They knew that to flee from that voice would be to flee from themselves. There have been people who have said to the voice: You and you alone are our God. There have been people who have offered themselves, in order to pass on this voice to others, by doing God. Only they pass that voice on. For it is while they are doing God that they see God.

Yes, there have been people who have known the worst—and it is at that moment that they awake. Their starting point seems absurd, that moment in which things could not be worse—death itself: Isaiah had a vision that all people should be free from oppression while he himself lived as a slave, captive by a foreign power. Martin Luther dreamed of a perfect Church as Jesus intended although he himself was persecuted by this Church and eventually excommunicated. Dietrich Bonhoeffer wrote about a God who is alive and living in his people while he lay helpless and captive in a concentration camp during World War II. Anne Frank, a young girl, whose diary stated, "In spite of everything, I still believe that people are really good at heart." She wrote those words while she was a fugitive from the Nazi massacre of the Jews during the Holocaust. Martin Luther King, Jr., had a dream of a world of peace and justice where blacks, whites, and all people could live in peace despite their differences. His dream was formed in our own time, a time of assassinations, fraud in government, and even in the Church. Harriet Tubman, herself an escaped slave, risked her life to free three hundred other black slaves from American white dominance. Francis of Assisi had the courage to live in poverty and without security and to challenge the church of his day that was steeped in power, dogmas, security, money, riches, land, and large buildings of gold and silver. John XXIII believed so much in the voice within that he called a council that made changes that even frightened him and his peers. Cardinal John Newman, who pierced the ghetto Catholic mentality of his day, to send priests to minister to students at non-Catholic colleges and universities. And then there is <u>Mother Teresa of Calcutta</u> who walked the streets in India past hundreds of thousands of people daily who build tiny fires to cook their scraps of food, defecate at curbstones, and curl up in their cotton rags against a wall to sleep and often to die. Above this scene of unremitting human desolation she and her many followers collected the dying from the streets so that they may leave life in peace among friends. And in our own country there was <u>Dorothy Day</u> who risked her own life for the poor fighting for justice and a better world, occasionally from a New York jail cell.

Yes, there are people, even today, who risk life itself to gain a better world. There are people who, even in the midst of conflict and war, have a vision of something new.

This vision and this voice offer no answers, no security, no power, no shelter, no riches. And yet there have been and are people who risk following their vision, this voice, because they have found it is not a fantasy, but a flesh-and-blood reality; that it can be done and was lived in one man to perfection. His name was Jesus and he came from a small town in Galilee called Nazareth. He had no power, no security, no roof over his head. He had no answers to give. He simply lived life. He took the risk and died many times. He yelled above the breakers in a sea of power, prestige—the super gods of his day—and spoke the courageous message that life is worth living no matter how hard it may be at times. People are worth living for even if at some point they kill us.

No matter who people are, he approaches them directly and asks: Who are you? What are you living for? Why aren't you living? And then he tells them, "You must be born anew, so must I. It can be yours— that kingdom of God, that new start—yours, with all your struggles for prestige, only if you are willing to become poor, a child; only if you are willing to recognize yourself in the least of people" (*At Times I see,* Huub Oosterhuis, Seabury press, 1974, page 62).

This is the risk you must take—the risk of recognizing yourself in others—to reach out at all costs—to be iron in the fire—to be water for the sea—a word for another. This is the risk taken by God himself, and there have been many people who have answered the call of this voice within themselves.

That same voice is speaking once again in **us**. That vision is growing once again within **us**. It loosens our tongues. It makes us share our lives. It has brought us here together.

That voice demands of us what it demanded of people since the beginning of time. First of all, there will be risks for us—the risk of becoming active and awake in a passive and dormant ecumenical malaise; the risk of understanding each other's views, backgrounds, and attitudes; the risk of being open, permissive, and loving without limits; the risk of trusting each other.

Secondly, we will have responsibilities—to respond to that voice; to broaden our vision and view of that voice to include more than Catholic or Lutheran or Christian; to be reborn, to have a reawakening to the possibilities of now and a hope for the future.

Finally, there is the vision itself—to see as God sees, to become prophetic; to remain diverse yet united; to learn to become other than we are and not be satisfied with just being; to seek wholeness (to be just Lutheran is only a part—to be just Roman Catholic is only a part—to be just Christian is only a part). Wholeness goes beyond Christianity to incorporate all people.

This conference is apocalyptic, for the future is happening now in us. The same future and vision which was begun in Jesus becomes present over and over again wherever people respond to that voice and that vision.

Have we responded to that voice? Can we handle this vision? The voice I speak of calls us light, salt, water, something new. Can we become this vision: water for the sea, light of the world, a word for another, salt of the earth?

I think we can! It's already beginning! Haven't you noticed!

27.

REFORMATION SUNDAY

(Delivered at Ascension Lutheran Church in Towson, Maryland on October 31, 1999.)

Readings: Jeremiah 31:31-34 Romans 3:19-28 John 8:31-36

This is the day when four histories will intersect in a most unique way!

This is the day when each of these four histories has something to teach the other three! This is the day the Lord has made, let us be glad and rejoice in it!

In Augsburg, Germany, in the City of Baltimore, and in numerous places like this around the globe, delegates from the Lutheran and Roman Catholic traditions will celebrate the signing of a definitive document that will bring our two traditions closer than ever before in history.

In fact, the signing of this document entitled, "Justification by Grace through Faith," is the very moment in which these four histories will converge as they never have before. The four histories I speak of are: my personal history as a Roman Catholic; your personal history as a Lutheran; my Catholic Church's history; and your Lutheran Church's history.

Both our Churches' histories traditionally begin in the year 1517 when a thirty-four-year-old Roman Catholic priest by the name of Father Martin posts his Ninety-five Theses on the door of Wittenberg's Castle Church in Germany. That (now historic) moment began a new world, a reform movement, a schism, an excommunication, the Diet of Augsburg, the Council of Trent, and over four hundred years of alienation and hostility between our two traditions.

At Augsburg (1530) and Trent (1545), the Western world watched as two members of the body of Christ verbally and at times physically abused one another. At Augsburg and Trent the Western world watched as two children of the same faith severed the ties that bind and went separate ways like the two brothers in the parable of the Prodigal Son. This is the history you and I were handed at birth, and most especially at our baptisms. We are living with the sins of history on both sides of this Christian story.

Now, you and I have our own personal histories, which have been clearly determined by these past four hundred years. Even though you are Lutheran and I am Roman Catholic, I'll wager a guess that our personal histories are somewhat similar. Let me tell you mine and see if anything resonates:

My Mother's side of the family is Roman Catholic, and my Dad's side of the family is Protestant. I say Protestant, because it was always difficult to pin them down—one time they were Methodist, another time Presbyterian, another time Lutheran (you get the picture!). I, however, was raised Roman Catholic from baptism onward. As a matter of fact, I never attended anything but Roman Catholic schools all my life right up to and including college (grad and post grad). Now that you see how Catholic I really am, you must also realize the attitude with which I was raised toward "Protestants."

Three incidents come to mind that will illustrate and might also ring some bells in your own history:

1) Being taught at home and in school, never to even walk in front of a Protestant church. We used to cross the street and walk on the other side whenever we approached a Protestant church.

2) One Sunday sermon, our pastor was talking about the "faults" of Protestants, and among them he listed the "fact" that Protestants don't use the whole Bible. As he said, they take out the parts they don't want.

3) The last incident happened in school one day when Sister Antonia asked the fifth grade class to raise their hands if they had a Bible at home. I was embarrassed, because we did not have one and was unable to raise my hand. Well, to my surprise, Sister said to those with their hands raised, "You shouldn't have a Bible in your home. That's what Protestants do and we Catholics do not." Well you can imagine my relief at knowing that I was in the "right."

I am sure that each of you sitting here can supply us with similar if not the same sort of stories from your childhood days. But, thank God, we have come a long way since those days.

Our more recent histories have been different: Lutherans watched as the Roman Catholic world entered the challenges and blessings of the Second Vatican Council—a council that even Martin Luther would have approved of! Many of you even adopted our pope at that time (Pope John XXIII). He was known as the "Protestant pope." At the Newman Center where I am director, students would often mistake our Lutheran pastor's office as mine, since in her office hung a gigantic portrait of Pope John. At the Newman Center, we have shared office space with Lutheran Campus Ministry for over thirty years.

We Catholics watched Lutherans as you struggled with your American amalgamation, and in recent years, your agreements with the Episcopal and Reformed Presbyterian churches. What history-forming events these have been! Only in the past thirty years have we come to learn more about each other, learn more from each other, and above all, learn more about what it means to BE CHURCH! And so you see, this is the day that all four of our histories converge as never before.

For me, I think, a new chapter opened in my life when I came to Towson University twenty years ago and ministered side by side, first with Pastor Andrea Hagen and now with Pastor Paul Collinson-Streng. We shared in each other's history, taught each other about the "other," learned from each other, loved one another, and on a very small level we have begun to heal the wound of centuries.

When Bishop Mocko was pastor here at Ascension Lutheran, he and I co-celebrated many weddings between Lutherans and Catholics. We helped each other come to grips with our past histories and tried to do the same for the couples we married.

And on the world scale, there has been a Lutheran Catholic Dialogue going on for over thirty years on the international, national, and local levels. The document being signed today is a product of the "good works" of these dialogues.

Where we go from here is both in our hands and in the hands of God. God spoke out in the year 1517 and in the year 1530 and in the year 1545. How well our ancestors listened to the voice of God is already the judgment of history. That history has not been a good one for the body of Christ. It is now time for a new covenant between our two traditions, a time of a new truth that will set us free from our estranged past and point us toward the future, a future that awaits us both in the new millennium.

God spoke again in our own time—at Vatican II (1965), and this is what the voice said:

> The restoration of unity among all Christians is one of the principal concerns of the Second Vatican Council. Christ the Lord founded one Church and one Church only...The Lord of Ages wisely and patiently follows out the plan of grace on our behalf, sinners that we are. In recent times more than ever before, he has been rousing divided Christians to remorse over their divisions and to a longing for unity. Everywhere large numbers have felt the impulse of this grace...for the restoration of unity among all Christians. This movement toward unity is called "ecumenical." Those who belong to it invoke the Triune God and confess Jesus as Lord and Savior, doing this not merely as individuals, but also as corporate bodies. For almost everyone regards the body in which he or she has heard the Gospel as his or her Church, and indeed, God's Church. All however, though in different ways, long for the one visible Church of God, a Church truly universal and set forth into the world that the world may be converted to the Gospel and so be saved, to the glory of God ("Decree on Ecumenism" paragraph #1).

Will we each, Lutheran and Catholic, live up to the document we sign today, and have enough "faith" to be justified, to be Christ for the world and bring the vision of God's voice to such a needy world as ours?

28.
THE TEMPLE—THE SYNAGOGUE—THE CHURCH

Readings: Ezekiel 43:1-2, 4-7 Psalm 84 I Corinthians 3:9-13,16-17 John 2:13-22

The Temple—built by human hands to house the divine presence.

The Temple—the locus of God's favor and presence in the land of Israel.

The Temple—gathering place for friends and nesting place for sparrows.

The Temple—existing before the world began, dwelling place of God on earth, destroyed by human hands.

Or was it?!

St. Paul tells the Corinthians—you are God's temple. The Spirit of God dwells in you.

The Evangelist John calls Jesus' Body—the temple that will rise after being destroyed.

In the history of Israel, there have been two temples. The first temple was conceived by King David and built by his son, King Solomon, about nine hundred years before Jesus. That first temple stood as the dwelling place of God in Jerusalem for four hundred years, before being destroyed by the Babylonians around 587 years before Jesus. It was this first temple that the Prophet Ezekiel speaks of above. Ezekiel, himself, was deported to Babylon ten years before the temple was destroyed. This Scripture was the vision he had of the temple while he was in exile in Babylon.

When the Jews returned from exile around 539 BCE they embarked on rebuilding the temple, but never completed it until the time of King

Herod the Great under the Romans around forty years before the birth of Jesus. Therefore, the temple that graced the skyline of Jerusalem at the time of Jesus and Paul was the second temple begun by Zerubbabel and completed by King Herod. This second temple, too, was destroyed around 70 CE by the Romans. And it is in reference to this action by the Romans that Jesus prefigures this destruction by overturning the money changers' tables, and the Evangelist, John, interprets as the death and resurrection of Jesus himself.

The destruction of both the first and second temples became cause for consternation in Israel. If God's dwelling on earth was in the temple, and if the temple was a sign of God's favor on Israel—now that it was destroyed, where was God to be found on earth?

In answer to that question about the first temple, during the exile Ezekiel began to gather the people into synagogues and form small communities built around reading Torah and experiencing Torah or God's word as a new presence and favor.

In the early Christian communities, after the destruction of the second temple, the Evangelists and apostles did the same by gathering people into house churches and began to discover God's presence in Jesus and eventually in themselves as they came to the realization that they were his body.

Both synagogues and churches became replacements for the two temples which had been destroyed.

Today, we celebrate the dedication of the Pope's church in Rome— St. John Lateran—which has been the "mother and head of all churches of Rome and the world" since the year 324 AD. It was the site of five ecumenical councils and is dedicated to St. John the Baptist.

This celebration today is an occasion for us to be reminded of what it means to be Church—the meaning of "Church," like its Hebrew counterpart "Synagogue," is both the place of gathering and the gathering itself. The building is the Church and we are the Church!

But unlike the town hall or the stadium or a theatre, the Church is the gathering place of the "called." We who gather have been called. We who are called, gather. "Called" by God, through baptism into Jesus Christ and confirmed by the Holy Spirit into a life-giving covenant both in this world and beyond.

With the Church we are pilgrims on this journey...
In the Church we belong...
Through the Church we receive eternal life.

This mystery is great—it is lived out in the covenant between God and Israel and the marriage between Christ and the Church. The greatness of this mystery for the Christian is that we are the Church; the Church is the body of Christ; the body of Christ subsists in the Roman Catholic tradition; and together with all other Christians and other religions of the world we have become the People of God—the dwelling place of God on earth!

The Church—built by human hands to house the divine presence.

The Church—the locus of God's favor and presence in all the lands on the earth.

The Church—gathering place for friends and nesting place for pigeons.

The Church—existing before the world began, dwelling place of God on earth, the body of Christ, once destroyed and now risen to new life!

29.
THE FOUR MARKS OF THE CHURCH

Readings: Acts 9:26-31 Psalm 85 I John 3:18-24 John 14:15-21

What is this "Church" being built up in the Acts of the Apostles? What is this "Church" that Jesus promises not to leave orphaned? What is this "Church" that is called: Roman, Lutheran, Methodist, Episcopal, Archdiocese, parish, campus ministry, and a host of other titles? What is this "Church" that gathers here and down the street and across the city and around the whole world every Sunday?

Vatican II described the Church first as a mystery, then as the People of God, then as a servant, a sign of the Kingdom, a pilgrim, and lastly as a hierarchical society.

The Nicene creed refers to the "Church" as one...holy...catholic... apostolic...These are what we call the "marks" of the Church—gifts that the Church must strive to realize ever more fully in its ongoing life.

Since no one homily could ever tackle completely the question—What is the Church?...Let us reflect on the four marks of the Church to help us understand what we must look for and what we must discover in any group that calls itself "Church." The four marks or gifts of the Church are: that it is one, holy, catholic, and apostolic.

The Church is "ONE"

The Church has many denominations, but has one faith, one Lord (Jesus Christ), one baptism and one God who is over all. It is this one Lord who comes to us when we are asleep, implants his name in us, plays with us and takes us for his bride. It is this one baptism that makes us into children who are born again and raised all over. It is this one faith that is forever and ever a surprise. The Church is one!

The Church is "HOLY"

The Church is given by God—has existed before the world began—not created by human hands, but by the Word of God come in the flesh—Jesus the Christ! It is an all-pervasive holiness that is present with us everywhere, living here among us. It is the holiness of one among us who is God of God, yet born of a human mother. It is a holy way of life, being patient, good, and loving. It is even sometimes a holiness we do not see, recognize, or know! The Church is holy!

The Church is "CATHOLIC"

The Church is essentially universal—no one is excluded—no one is forgotten—multiethnic, multiracial, multicultural—no one is left out, not even the dead. No one language renders the Church. No one song can capture the Church. No one society can equal the unique catholicity of the Church. The Church is the future awaiting us, the past completed, a present, hopeful, peaceful body that lives. The Church is catholic!

The Church is "APOSTOLIC"

Like the apostles, the Church is sent—it has a mission to bring Christ to the world. The Church's mission is not to bring the world to Christ—not to convert, not to proselytize, but to serve the world with Good News. The Good News is that love has been, is, and will be the world's salvation. Mercy and faithful love will meet when the world meets the Church. Truth and peace will embrace one another when the Church embraces the world. The Church is faithfulness sprouting like seed in the earth. The Church is apostolic!

Many people today go "church shopping," looking for a church that best suits them. Instead—go in search of **the Church**—and you will recognize her by her four marks: One, holy, catholic, apostolic.

Once you have found **the Church**, bear with her feeble gestures, dwell in her as in a home, take her as your bride, remain in communion with her your whole life, for she has the words of eternal life!

(Many of the images used in this homily were taken from three texts by Huub Oosterhuis:

"The Lord Has Seen Me," "God with Us," and "Of Today and Tomorrow.")

30.
EVANGELIZATION

Readings: Jonah 3:1-5, 10 Psalm 30 Mark 1:14-22

If I were to ask you to define "evangelization," there would probably be as many definitions as there are people reading this homily. Even when the term "evangelization" is used by the experts, even then it is given a variety of meanings. Despite all this confusion, I have chosen to use this term "evangelization," and hope to offer it some meaning for the "Ecumenical Christian."

Let us begin with the Scripture to help us form a definition. In the passage from the Prophet Jonah, God calls Jonah to go and "evangelize" the great city of Nineveh. In other words, Jonah was called to bring God's word to the people of Nineveh; from this passage you can conclude that the people of Nineveh were great sinners in need of repentance. When they repented, God relented and did not destroy this great city of sinners. Through "evangelization" Jonah convinced the people to repent and become open to God's mercy rather than God's wrath.

We have traditionally called Mark and the other three authors of the Gospels "Evangelists"...The four Evangelists: Matthew, Mark, Luke, and John. In the Gospel above, Mark cites Jesus doing the same as John the Baptist, "evangelizing" the people of his day by asking them to reform their lives.

Jonah, Mark, John, and Jesus were all evangelizing even though we have traditionally only called one of them an Evangelist (Mark). Jonah, we call a prophet; John, we call the Baptist; and Jesus, we call Messiah. Yet all four men were in the business of "evangelization."

What precisely can we point to in all four of their techniques that would make us call what they did "evangelization"?

There is one common word that we find each of them using as the basis of their activity. That word is "believe" or "faith!" When the people of Nineveh "believed" God, then God relented. When John the Baptist called for repentance, he asked people to "believe" in the Good News. Notice how Mark has the first apostles respond to Jesus' call to "Come after me and I will make you fishers of people." They dropped everything and followed Jesus. In other words, they "believed" in Jesus. They were examples of what John the Baptist called for—belief in the Good News—Jesus is the Good News!

All four "Evangelists" (if I may be so bold to call them), brought people to *faith* in God. One aspect, then, of evangelization is to bring people to *faith*; to a fuller richer life of *faith*; to make the Good News of salvation known; to show people that life can be better and is worth living. Jonah, the Prophet; and Mark, the Evangelist; and John, the Baptist; and Jesus, the Messiah are still doing that today as they call each of us to an even greater faith and hope in God's Good News. They do it through God's Word, which we call the Bible. Every time we hear that word sound in our midst, Jonah and Mark and John and Jesus go where no roads go, but only word and faith go—into the minds and hearts of people. Their words and their stories have become the Word of God—a word that frees, liberates, and saves people from the bondage of sin and destruction. Together, they form the sacred Scripture, along with so many others who call all who have open hearts and minds to do the same. As God called Jonah, so Jonah calls Nineveh. As God called John, so John calls Israel. As God called Jesus, so Jesus calls apostles. As God called Mark, so Mark calls us. And if Mark is calling us, then God is calling us. And if God is calling us...who are we going to call?

I believe there are plenty of people in our lives who need us to call them back from deep pits of despair, lack of direction, and purposeless living. I believe there are people in our lives who are waiting for us to draw them up out of the graves of peer pressure, family pressure, and guilt trips. There are so many alive people who get numbered among the dead through drugs, alcohol, and sexual promiscuity. There are many calling out: "Help me, God!...Make me beautiful!...What use is it to you if I die?" We find them everywhere: Our friends, our roommates, our parents, our brothers or sisters, our children, our professors, our students, those we love.

One problem we face, however, is our inability to deal with them; our fear of the consequence if we do; our lack of experience in relating to someone's problems; our apathy at not wanting to rock the boat; our excuses that it's neither my problem nor my job to be concerned with this...leave it to the priest. Sometimes we even feel helpless and useless. Sometimes we lack confidence and courage. Sometimes we feel we lack even the authority.

The Gospel tells us that Jesus healed and taught with authority, with courage and confidence. His audience was spellbound by the determination with which he attacked the evil of his day. And you remember in another place in this same Gospel people remarked: "Where did he get all this?... Is he not the carpenter, the son of Mary" (Mark 6:2-3)?

Every one of us is someone's son or daughter. Every one of us feels incompetent to relate to people's problems. Every one of us fears exposure or rejection or failure if we don't succeed.

The whole message of evangelization is to help you see that, as Cardinal Newman once said, "Nothing would be done at all if a person waited till he could do it so well that no one could find fault with it."

You are competent because you are human! You are useful because you can care! You have the authority of the Church who baptized you to do precisely these things. As to the confidence and courage—no one can give you these. These are yours to seek out. These are yours to acquire. These you must find in yourself by evangelizing yourself. Every Christian is asked to begin with themselves.

Evangelize myself?—What does that mean?

Here are a few suggestions for you to ponder and reflect on as you begin the process to evangelize yourself:

- to evaluate where you are, where you have been, where you are going...
- to strengthen what is already...
- to become more aware of what's out there, what's in here...
- to take stock of yourself...
- to preach to yourself...
- to open up to God in your life...
- to rejuvenate your faith...
- to stir up the still-burning embers...
- to reawaken what is dormant...
- to search for what is lost...
- to grow beyond where you are now...
- to learn again...
- to teach yourself...
- to go back to school...
- to progress toward some goal...
- to revive your fervor and zeal...
- to bring to life that which has died...
- to recognize what is new...
- to believe again in the old...
- to be reborn...
- to restore all that is good...
- to renew the covenant of your baptism...

May I add one final aspect to the theme of evangelization before I let you alone to contemplate the above list of suggestions?

Evangelization or evangelizing ourselves doesn't mean to do *more* than we are already doing—but to do what we are already doing *better*!

Evangelization is doing what we do already and being who we are already, but doing it and being it *better* than we have been...with greater zeal and commitment.

Evangelization means *better* and not necessarily *more*.

The American value that "more is better" might have invaded our attempts to become better Christians.

Adding more things to do to our already busy world might be defeating the purpose we have in mind.

Perhaps we should be looking at things to cut out rather than add to our life as a Christian.

Often when we strip away the baggage, we can get to the heart of the matter more easily. If there is a need to *add more*—let it be **zeal** and **commitment!**

Do what Jesus did—he began with himself ("forty days in the desert")—then he went to those around him ("the lost sheep of Israel")—and then he created a community to help him ("on this rock I will build my Church")—and that's **us—the Church!**

Made in the USA